Public Sector Technology Transfer

For Carol, who makes every day beautiful!

Public Sector Technology Transfer

Albert N. Link

Virginia Batte Phillips Distinguished Professor of Economics,
University of North Carolina at Greensboro, USA

Edward **Elgar**
PUBLISHING

Cheltenham, UK • Northampton, MA, USA

Published by
Edward Elgar Publishing Limited
The Lypiatts
15 Lansdown Road
Cheltenham
Glos GL50 2JA
UK

Edward Elgar Publishing, Inc.
William Pratt House
9 Dewey Court
Northampton
Massachusetts 01060
USA

A catalogue record for this book
is available from the British Library

Library of Congress Control Number: 2023952098

This book is available electronically in the **Elgar**online
Business subject collection
http://dx.doi.org/10.4337/9781035310531

ISBN 978 1 0353 1052 4 (cased)
ISBN 978 1 0353 1053 1 (eBook)

Printed and bound in Great Britain by
TJ Books Limited, Padstow, Cornwall

Contents

Figures

Tables

About the author

Albert N. Link is the Virginia Batte Phillips Distinguished Professor of Economics at the University of North Carolina at Greensboro (UNCG). He received the B.S. degree in mathematics from the University of Richmond (Phi Beta Kappa) and the Ph.D. degree in economics from Tulane University. After receiving the Ph.D., he joined the economics faculty at Auburn University, was later Scholar-in-Residence at Syracuse University, and then he joined the economics faculty at UNCG in 1982. In 2019, Link was awarded the title and honorary position of Visiting Professor at Northumbria University, U.K.

Professor Link's research focuses on technology and innovation policy, the economics of R&D, and policy/program evaluation. He is currently the Editor-in-Chief of the *Journal of Technology Transfer*. He is also co-editor of *Foundations and Trends in Entrepreneurship* and founder/editor of *Annals of Science and Technology Policy*.

Among his more than 70 authored and edited books, some of the more recent ones are: *The Economics and Science of Measurement: A Study of Metrology* (Routledge, 2022), *Technology and Innovation Policy: An International Perspective* (Edward Elgar, 2021), *Invention, Innovation and U.S. Federal Laboratories* (Edward Elgar, 2020), *Technology Transfer and U.S. Public Sector Innovation* (Edward Elgar, 2020), *Collaborative Research in the United States: Policies and Institutions for Cooperation among Firms* (Routledge, 2020), *Sources of Knowledge and Entrepreneurial Behavior* (University of Toronto Press, 2019), *Handbook for University Technology Transfer* (University of Chicago Press, 2015), *Public Sector Entrepreneurship: U.S. Technology and Innovation Policy* (Oxford University Press, 2015), *Bending the Arc of Innovation: Public Support of R&D in Small, Entrepreneurial Firms* (Palgrave Macmillan, 2013), *Valuing an Entrepreneurial Enterprise* (Oxford University Press, 2012), *Public Goods, Public Gains: Calculating the Social Benefits of Public R&D* (Oxford University Press, 2011), *Employment Growth from Public Support of Innovation in Small Firms* (W.E. Upjohn Institute for Employment Research, 2011), and *Government as Entrepreneur* (Oxford University Press, 2009).

Professor Link's other research endeavors consist of more than 250 peer-reviewed journal articles and book chapters, as well as numerous U.S. government reports. His scholarship has appeared in such academic journals as the *American Economic Review*, the *Journal of Political Economy*, the

Review of Economics and Statistics, Economica, Research Policy, Economics of Innovation and New Technology, the *European Economic Review, Small Business Economics, ISSUES in Science and Technology, Science and Public Policy, Scientometrics,* and the *Journal of Technology Transfer.*

Professor Link's public service includes being a member of the National Research Council's research team that conducted the 2010 evaluation of the U.S. Small Business Innovation Research (SBIR) program. Based on that assignment, he testified before the U.S. Congress in April 2011 on the economic benefits associated with the SBIR program. Link also served from 2007 to 2012 as a U.S. Representative to the United Nations (in Geneva, Switzerland) in the capacity of co-vice chairperson of the Team of Specialists on Innovation and Competitiveness Policies Initiative for the Economic Commission for Europe. In October 2018, Link delivered the European Commission Distinguished Scholar Lecture at the European Commission's Joint Research Centre (in Seville, Spain).

Currently, Link is an active member of the National Institute of Standards and Technology funded research team studying the economic impacts of investments in U.S. neutron research sources and facilities, and an advisor to the research team focusing on the SBIR program in the National Heart, Lung, and Blood Institute within the Department of Health and Human Services.

Foreword

Paul Zielinski

Every day we use a multitude of technologies that have increasingly defined both how we live and who we are. From the earliest days, research has led to improvements in the tools we use, and the importance of innovation has grown as tools have become more technologically sophisticated. The term *innovation* is often used to describe things that are new, but to be truly innovative, a clever idea must also be useful and something people want to buy and use. This creation of value is what leads to economic growth.

The increasing pace of discovery and even innovation has provided a sound framework and case for technology transfer. After a long career in government spanning seven Administrations, I have seen the transformative power of new technologies in many areas such as alternative energy sources in addition to the more obvious changes in electronics and artificial intelligence. Even space travel is no longer simply a government endeavor but also a commercial one. While there are many areas of disagreement in politics, the idea that advances in technology and innovation lead to prosperity seems to be one of the few that has broad support.

From a government or university point of view, science and research are interesting and often produce academic works. These advance thinking and continue to expand our understanding. The Bayh-Dole Act of 1980 has been lauded as a critical catalyst for the commercialization of new technology. The idea is as simple as it is brilliant: allowing the developers of government-funded research to obtain intellectual property rights and have an active role in the success of a product greatly multiplies the number of people moving an innovation forward.

Laboratories only move technology so far, and that is far short of the idea of value creation. As of this writing, the National Science Foundation's (NSF) federal expenditure in research and development is over $180 billion annually. That is a sizeable investment, but at the most fundamental mission level, this large investment is all sitting on the shelf. That's because, in a capitalist nation, the government generally does not make or sell consumer products or services. Even in defense, acquisition efforts are incredibly important because weapon systems are bought—not made—by the government.

As I note when talking about federal technology transfer efforts, the success of technology transfer is measured by the success of private partners to make and sell the results of R&D. It's the private sector, not the government, that uses this enabling research to make commercial products that you buy. Moving innovative ideas from the bench to the store shelf keeps the U.S. economy vibrant and nimble in an ever-more-competitive world.

Still, even the sizeable funding the government spends on research is nowhere close to enough to bring products to market and fuel economic growth. Bridging that gap requires private investment. NSF notes that private R&D funding outpaces government investment by more than two-fold. Much of this money is specifically for advancing innovative products to a final marketable form. Despite all the capabilities and ideas at government and university laboratories, the federal R&D investment relies on American businesses and private investment to see new products and services reach the marketplace and create the jobs of the future. The results of this transition from research labs to the private sector are apparent in products that are all around us. Numerous pharmaceuticals that originated in labs at the National Institutes of Health (NIH) prevent and treat diseases spanning from HIV to cancer to Lyme disease. Even the internet itself is well known as a product of the Defense Advanced Research Projects Agency (DARPA). There are tremendous opportunities, and strong partnerships are needed to lead to true innovation.

Although the government and even universities can seem distant and looming, operating within the proverbial "ivory tower," in reality they are very open to working with businesses of all sizes. Far from being a distraction, these partnerships represent an important part of the lifecycle for any research effort. While labs certainly have advanced the general scientific understanding in key areas, this collaborative work makes a difference in people's lives every day. The process of transferring technology and innovation from our laboratory through a variety of mechanisms is both a mission and a priority for these organizations.

With all of these ideas coming from hundreds of federal labs, finding partners to work with and identifying what ideas exist can seem like an impossible task. And because it's not a one-size-fits-all world, technology transfer offices need to be flexible and meet the needs of prospective partners. Organizations like the Federal Laboratory Consortium (FLC) or the Association of University Technology Managers (AUTM) can help as nodes that collect and provide cross-organization information and contacts to facilitate collaborations.

In the Obama and Trump White House this effort was labeled the Lab to Market Cross Agency Priority Goal. There was a recognition that government or universities funded by government grants will need private investment to complete the delivery of a product. Traditionally, this reliance on private investment and the market picking "the winners" has been a strength of the

U.S. economy when it comes to technology development and transfer. But that dynamic is being tested like never before.

While the United States has enjoyed tremendous success in technology transfer, thanks in large part to the Bayh-Dole Act, the system is showing its age. Now, over 40 years later, the world around us is quite different from the 1980s. Global competition and markets are now normal as ecommerce shortens distances. New competitors and markets in Asia have even shaken the traditional dominance of the U.S. economy in driving technology. Simply put, a U.S. patent does not provide the same level of competitive advantage for market entry that it did just a short time ago. And, increasingly, patents often are not quick enough to keep up with the lifecycle of digital products.

Even the traditional notion of inventorship is reaching its end. With artificial intelligence encroaching on so many aspects of our lives, the definitions of creation and even the conception of an idea are evolving.

Similarly, the "click economy" as an alternative to the more traditional develop and sell pathway has had a significant impact. Under a more traditional model, a product is made, offered for sale and purchased with the maker/seller earning a profit. In the click economy, offering vast amounts of information for "free" generates profit through curation. This establishes a tension between creators and platforms that are more focused on increasing throughput to data.

Given the major shifts in how ideas become products and how these products reach the market, a book like this is critical to continue to expand thinking. We cannot expect the tools from decades ago—which were designed before we even understood these technologies and market dynamics—to continue to meet demand. However, they do lay a solid foundation upon which to build, or at the least a contrast to explore a competitive advantage.

It is critical that we continue to challenge the past with new ideas, study the effectiveness of technology transfer and consider next steps. Perhaps some fundamental shifts are needed, or maybe the foundations will continue to stand up to the storm with minor changes. In either case, a purposeful and complete examination and continued evaluation is needed for expanding our understanding and for developing the next generation of tools. We will easily be surpassed in the field of technology transfer—as in any other endeavor—if we do not continue to innovate.

Paul Zielinski
Executive Director
Federal Laboratory Consortium for Technology Transfer (FLC)

Preface

This book represents the culmination of decades of research and writing about public sector technology transfer where the term *public sector* refers to U.S. government agencies and laboratories.

My interest in this subject came from my early work supported through research awards from the Department of Energy and from the National Institute of Standards and Technology (NIST). A few of the chapters in this book relate to technology transfers by small firms funded through the Small Business Innovation Research (SBIR) program and the Small Business Technology Transfer (STTR) program. My interest in the activities of technology-based small firms came, in part, from my involvement with the STEP Board of the National Academies during its first Congressionally sponsored survey of Phase II SBIR projects. As such, this book builds on many of my previous experiences and publications.

Because part of this book relates to institutional and legislative history, some duplication of text material is inevitable. Also, because part of this book might become a reference source for some, I have quoted extensively from public sector legislation and policy documents.

Acknowledgments

A grateful thank you to the National Research Council of the U.S. National Academies of Sciences, Engineering, and Medicine for making available the data analyzed in several chapters of this book. I am also grateful to Now Publishers for the transfer of the copyright of Link (2022b) to me; positions of that manuscript are included in this book.

My sincere thanks also go to all of the individuals at Edward Elgar Publishing who were involved throughout the conceptualization stage, the review process, and the publication process. My sincere thanks too to Farhat Chowdhury for her efforts to seam together the chapters in this book, as well as to the anonymous reviewers who offered insightful comments and suggestions on earlier drafts.

Finally, the support of my loving wife, as this project progressed, has been invaluable. This book is appropriately dedicated to her.

Abbreviations

AAAS	American Association for the Advancement of Science
AIA	America Invents Act
ANC	Alaskan Native Corporation
ARRA	American Recovery and Reinvestment Act
CAP	Cross agency priority
CRADA	Cooperative Research and Development Agreement
CRS	Congressional Research Service
D	Democrat
D	Development
DC	District of Columbia
DHS	Department of Homeland Security
DOC	Department of Commerce
DOD	Department of Defense
DOE	Department of Energy
DOI	Department of the Interior
DOT	Department of Transportation
EC	European Commission
EPA	Educational partnership agreement
EPA	Environmental Protection Agency
FCRC	Federal Contract Research Center
FFRDC	Federally Funded Research and Development Center
FLC	Federal Laboratory Consortium
FY	Fiscal year
GOCO	Government owned and contractor operated
GOGO	Government owned and government operated
HHS	Health and Human Services

IAWGTT	Interagency Workgroup/Working Group on Technology Transfer
IPPM	Intellectual property protection mechanism
JTT	*Journal of Technology Transfer*
K	Capital
KT	Knowledge transfer/s
L	Labor
M	Millions of dollars
MA	Massachusetts
MD	Maryland
MFP	Multifactor productivity
MIT	Massachusetts Institute of Technology
MTA	Material transfer agreement
NACA	National Advisory Committee for Aeronautics
NASA	National Aeronautics and Space Administration
NBER	National Bureau of Economic Research
NBS	National Bureau of Standards
NH	New Hampshire
NHO	Native Hawaiian Organization
NIH	National Institutes of Health
NIST	National Institute of Standards and Technology
NRC	National Research Council
NSF	National Science Foundation
NTIS	National Technical Information Service
ORM	Office of Research Materials
ORTA	Office of Research and Technology Applications
OSRD	Office of Scientific Research and Development
OSTP	Office of Science and Technology Policy
OTA	Office of Technology Assessment
OTS	Office of Technical Services
OUSDR&E	Office of the Under Secretary of Defense for Research and Engineering
PCT	Patent Cooperation Treaty

PIA	Partnership intermediary agreement
PMA	President's Management Agenda
PRO	Publicly funded research organization
Q	Output
R	Research
R&D	Research and development
RCA	Research collaboration agreement
ROI	Return on investment
S&E	Science and engineering
SBA	Small Business Administration
SBC	Small business concern
SBIR	Small Business Innovation Research program
SRM	Standard Reference Material
STEM	Science, technology, engineering, and mathematics
STTR	Small Business Technology Transfer program
T2	Technology transfer
TT	Technology transfer
U.K.	United Kingdom
UNCG	University of North Carolina at Greensboro
UNESCO	United Nations Educational, Scientific and Cultural Organization
U.S.	United States
U.S.C.	U.S. Code
USDA	United States Department of Agriculture
USDOC	U.S. Department of Commerce
USPTO	U.S. Patent and Trademark Office
VA	Department of Veterans Affairs
WV	West Virginia

1. Why public sector technology transfer?

SETTING THE STAGE

The question posed in the title of this introductory chapter is intended to evoke one or both of the following responses: Why is the public sector (i.e., national or federal government) involved in technology transfer? Why is technology transfer important? The answer to each of these questions is simple ... *technology transfer can occur for the common good*!

To quote from President Barack Obama's 2011 Presidential Memorandum—Accelerating Technology Transfer and Commercialization of Federal Research in Support of High-Growth Businesses:

> Innovation fuels economic growth, the creation of new industries, companies, jobs, products and services, and the global competitiveness of U.S. industries. One driver of successful innovation is technology transfer ...

And to quote from President Donald Trump's President's Management Agenda (undated, p. 49), his administration sought to:

> Improve the transfer of technology from federally funded research and development to the private sector to promote U.S. economic growth and national security.

Thus, the purpose of this book is to provide analytical information (i.e., descriptive trends and statistical relationships) to characterize U.S. public sector technology transfer activities—activities that are publicly funded and publicly performed as well as those that are publicly funded and privately performed.

One generally thinks that public sector intervention into market activity is justified on the basis of market failure. In the case of private sector investments (by the firm) in research (the R in R&D—research and development), which could possibly lead to a new technology, it might be the case that the firm underinvests from a social perspective in such research because of research risk and market uncertainty. Risk and uncertainty can lead to the firm's inability to appropriate all of the benefits from research allocations.

Following Link and Scott (2011), there are at least eight categories of risk and uncertainty-related investment and market barriers that the private sector firm faces when making investments in R&D. These non-mutually exclusive categories can result in the expected private rate of return to the firm being less than the desired social rate of return from the use of such R&D resources. These categories include: high technical risk; high human capital costs; a long time to complete the R&D project and commercialize the resulting technology; the underlying R&D spilling over to multiple markets and, thus, not being appropriable; the fact that the market success of the technology depends on the development of technologies in different industries; conditions when property rights cannot be assigned to the underlying R&D; an environment where resulting technology must be compatible and interoperable with other technologies; and the presence of opportunistic behavior when sharing information about the technology.[1] Individually, or in combination, these investment and related barriers to the potential development and marketability of any resulting technology will lead the private sector firm to underinvest in R&D from the perspective of society. When, from a social perspective, there is this underinvestment in research knowledge[2]—and knowledge is a public good[3]—by the private sector, a market failure has occurred and thus, there can be an appropriate role for the public sector to intervene through policy initiatives.[4]

Does market failure explain the public sector's involvement in technology transfer? The answer to this question is perhaps more nuanced than the answer for private sector R&D.

The idea or belief that an appropriate role for the public sector is to, among other things, transfer public sector technology and technical knowledge throughout the economy traces not to the concept of market failure but rather directly to the Founding Fathers of the U.S. Constitution (Link and Wagner, 2021).[5,6] In particular, Article I, Section 8 of the Constitution states the following:

> The Congress shall have the power ... To *promote* [emphasis added] the progress of *science and useful arts* [emphasis added], by securing for limited times to authors and inventors the exclusive right to their respective *writings and discoveries* [emphasis added].[7]

Following Link and Wagner (2021), nowhere in the Constitution is it defined which specific "science and useful arts" should be promoted by the Congress; nowhere in the Constitution is there a blueprint for what "writings and discoveries" are in the country's best interest. Perhaps the Founding Fathers, in their wisdom, realized that science and the useful arts change over time through writings and discoveries. Perhaps, too, the Founding Fathers used the verb *promote* rather than the verb *direct* to underscore their view of government having an *indirect role* in such pursuits (although there are examples of the government having a *direct role* in instances when there was perceived to be market failures related to optimal level of investments or the removal of market barriers that inhibited the private sector from identifying what to write about or what needs to be discovered). The indirect versus direct role of government has been debated over the years. Still, the verb *promote* implicitly suggests a process of transfer.

Link and Wagner (2021, pp. 757, 761), drawing on UNESCO (1968), wrote the following about instances where the U.S. government pursued an indirect as well as a direct method to support discovery:

> There are counterexamples in America's early history of an indirect role of government in the creation of knowledge. For example, President (Thomas) Jefferson believed that at times the role of the government should be direct. For example, he, as President, sponsored the Lewis and Clark expedition in 1803 with the intent of advancing geographic knowledge and "the *promotion* [emphasis added] of the general welfare depended heavily upon advances in scientific knowledge." In 1838, President (Martin) van Buren similarly took the position of the government having a direct role in the support of technological knowledge. Samuel Morse had demonstrated the feasibility of the electric telegraph, and, thus, the van Buren Congress awarded Morse $30,000 to build an experimental telegraphic line between Baltimore, Maryland, and Washington, DC.

With regard to these referenced examples, Link (2006) has argued that the Lewis and Clark expedition possibly represents the first instance of public support of pure or basic research, whereas Morse's telegraphic line possibly represents the first instance of publicly supported applied research. One might also argue that the geography-related knowledge learned by Lewis and Clark had at the time, and even now, the characteristics of being a public good, and the public sector appropriated only portions of the knowledge that the public sector *promoted* and funded. Finally, the telegraphic line that Morse constructed was owned by the government, but the spillover knowledge from that new technology (i.e., the use of this new technology) was not accessible to everyone, only to those who paid a usage fee.

Seely (2008, p. 5) identified another example of the government having a direct role in the development of a new technology:

> … the federal government played a … direct role in advancing industrial research and disseminating knowledge. In March 1915, Congress had authorized formation of the National Advisory Committee on Aeronautics (NACA) to help overcome the technical challenges of developing military aircraft. Finding the U.S. Army well behind the Germans, French, and British in this field of military and industrial technology, members of Congress agreed to fund a committee of leading experts from industry and universities to guide federal research and development efforts in the aviation field.

The debate about the government having an indirect versus a direct role in the support of a new technology and new technical knowledge gained a voice in the 1940s through the public and written debates between Vannevar Bush and Senator Harley Kilgore (WV, D). Bush was in favor of universities being the centerpiece of U.S. science policy whereas Kilgore favored less autonomy for a scientific research agenda being set by scientists.[8]

HISTORICAL CONTEXT

The Stevenson-Wydler Act of 1980

For historical context about the transfer of new or existing technology and technical knowledge, one might point to the years immediately following World War II during which several government agencies (e.g., the Department of Defense (DOD) and the National Institute of Health, later the National Institutes of Health (NIH)), exerted their authority not to share their internally financed basic research activities.[9] Following Link and Wagner (2021), other agencies similarly followed a so-called protective policy about their R&D efforts. Such protective behavior was curtailed in June 1945 when President Harry Truman signed Executive Order 9568, which created the Publication Board and which allowed for scientific information, which may be of benefit to the public, to be released.[10] Later that year, the Publication Board was merged into the Office of Technical Services (OTS) within the Department of Commerce (DOC) (Stewart, 1993). In 1950, Congress passed the Research and Technical Services Act (Public Law 81–776), which gave authority for what would eventually become the National Technical Information Service (NTIS). Specifically, the 1950 act states:

> The Secretary of Commerce … is hereby directed to establish and maintain within the Department of Commerce a clearinghouse for the collection and dissemination of scientific, technical, and engineering information, and to this end to take such steps as he may deem necessary and desirable … [t]o make such information available to industry and business, to State and local governments, to other agencies of the Federal Government, and to the general public …

And the trend toward openness to public sector funded research continued. Many view the first legislation that was specific to the transfer of codified publicly funded research and technical knowledge came with the passage of the Stevenson-Wydler Act of 1980. The Federal Laboratory Consortium (FLC, discussed in detail in Chapter 4) declared in *The Green Book* that the Stevenson-Wydler Act is (FLC, 2018, p. xi) "the first of a continuing series of laws to define and promote technology transfer," followed by the Federal Technology Transfer Act of 1986.

Table 1.1 lists key technology transfer-related legislation, as identified by the FLC. Many of the entries in the table are explicitly focused on public sector technology transfer while others focus on public sector knowledge transfer (e.g., tacit and codified intellectual property), the latter being the subject of Chapter 2. The Stevenson-Wydler Act of 1980 is prominent in the table, as is the Federal Technology Transfer Act of 1986. While it might be argued that the Stevenson-Wydler Act represented the logical progression of post-World War II thinking about publicly funded R&D, Leyden and Link (2015) placed that legislation, among other legislation, as being a response to the productivity slowdown that began in the United States in the early 1970s and regained its steam in the late 1970s and early 1980s.[11]

Table 1.1   Recent technology transfer-related legislation

Legislation	Summary
Stevenson-Wydler Technology Innovation Act of 1980 (Public Law 96–480)	Required federal laboratories to allocate a percentage of the laboratory's budget to technology transfer activities, and each laboratory must establish an Office of Research and Technology Applications (ORTA) to promote technology transfer.
Bayh-Dole Act of 1980 (Public Law 96–517)	Allowed small businesses, universities, and not-for-profit organizations title to inventions developed with federal funds, thus these organizations could transfer federally funded technologies through patent licenses. Government owned and government operated (GOGO) laboratories were permitted to grant exclusive patent licenses to commercial organizations.
Small Business Innovation Development Act of 1982 (Public Law 97–219)	Required federal agencies with extramural research budgets above a threshold amount to set aside a portion of those funds for small businesses (less than 500 employees). Funded organizations transfer federally funded technologies through patent licenses and publications.
Federal Technology Transfer Act of 1986 (Public Law 99–502)	Required federal laboratory scientists and engineers to consider technology transfer an individual responsibility, and such actions are a part of his/her performance evaluations. The law permitted government owned, government operated (GOGO) laboratories to participate in Cooperative Research and Development Agreements (CRADAs) and to form licensing agreements for patented inventions from cooperative research and development.
Executive Order 12591, Facilitating Access to Science and Technology (1987)	Through President Ronald Regan's authority, federal laboratories and agencies were to transfer relevant technical knowledge to universities and private sector organizations.
Omnibus Trade and Competitiveness Act of 1988 (Public Law 100–418)	Emphasized the benefits to research and development (R&D) from public/private cooperation in centers for manufacturing technology such as Industrial Extension Services. The National Bureau of Standards (NBS) was renamed the National Institute of Standards and Technology (NIST) and its technology was broadened to be the FLC's host agency.

Legislation	Summary
National Competitiveness Technology Transfer Act of 1989 (Public Law 101–189)	Permitted government owned and contractor operated (GOCO) laboratories to enter into CRADAs in like manner as GOGO laboratories as legislated by the Federal Technology Transfer Act of 1986.
American Technology Preeminence Act of 1991 (Public Law 102–245)	Allowed federal laboratories to contribute intellectual property to industry under CRADA arrangements.
Small Business Research and Development Enhancement Act of 1992 (Public Law 102–564)	Established the Small Business Technology Transfer (STTR) program similar to the Small Business Innovation Research (SBIR) program with the added purpose of facilitating the transfer of technology developed through the small firm's collaboration with a research institute partner.
National Department of Defense Authorization Act for 1994 (Public Law 103–160)	Broadened the definition of a federal laboratory to include Department of Energy (DOE) weapons production facilities.
National Technology Transfer and Advancement Act of 1995 (Public Law 104–113)	Amended the Stevenson-Wydler Act to make CRADAs more attractive to both federal laboratories and scientists and to private industry by assuring that U.S. companies will be granted intellectual property rights to justify prompt commercialization of inventions arising from a CRADA with a federal laboratory.
Technology Transfer Commercialization Act of 2000 (Public Law 106–404)	Permitted federal laboratories to grant a license for a federally owned invention created/dated before an existing CRADA began.
Energy Policy Act of 2005 (Public Law 109–58)	Established in the Department of Energy (DOE) a technology transfer coordinator to be the principal advisor to the Secretary of Energy on technology transfer and technology commercialization; a working group at the DOE laboratories on technology transfer matters; and an energy technology commercialization fund for matching funds with private organizations to promote energy technologies for commercial purposes.
America Creating Opportunities to Meaningfully Promote Excellence in Technology, Education, and Science Act of 2007 (America COMPETES Act, Public Law 110–69)	Authorized programs to increase funding for basic research; to strengthen teacher capabilities and encourage student opportunities in science, technology, engineering, and mathematics (STEM) educational programs; and enhance support for higher risk, higher reward research, all of which are cornerstones of enhancing those capable of promoting technology transfer activities and using transferred technologies.
Leahy–Smith America Invents Act of 2011 (AIA, Public Law 112–29)	Changed the patent system from a first to invent system to a first to file system bringing the U.S. patent system in line with much of the rest of the world.

Source: Based on FLC (2018).

As written in the Stevenson-Wydler Act:

> The Congress finds and declares that: Technology and industrial innovation are central to the economic, environmental, and social well-being of citizens of the United States. Technology and industrial innovation offer an improved standard of living, increased public and private sector productivity, creation of new industries and employment opportunities, improved public services and enhanced competitiveness of United States products in world markets. Many new discoveries and advances in science occur in ... Federal laboratories, while the application of this new knowledge to commercial and useful public purposes depends largely upon actions by business and labor ... The Federal laboratories and other performers of federally funded research and development frequently provide scientific and technological developments of potential use to State and local governments and private industry. These developments should be made accessible to those governments and industry.

One might also interpret this last sentence from the Stevenson-Wydler Act as a statement of fact that thus is a motivation for the direct sharing of technology and its embodied knowledge. The Act continued:

> There is a need to provide means of access and to give adequate personnel and funding support to these means ... It is the purpose of this Act to improve the economic, environmental, and social well-being of the United States by ... promoting technology development through the establishment of centers for industrial technology [within federal laboratories and] stimulating improved utilization of federally funded technology developments by State and local governments and the private sector ...

One might interpret these last few statements to mean that there is a public sector response to the private sector's failure to invest sufficiently in technology-based resources. And the remaining sentences from the Act assert that the public sector must undertake the task of alleviating this private sector market failure.[12]

> It is the continuing responsibility of the Federal Government to ensure the full use of the results of the Nation's Federal investment in research and development. To this end the Federal Government shall strive where appropriate to transfer Federally owned or originated technology to State and local governments and to the private sector.

One might note that there are themes within the above excerpt from the Stevenson-Wydler Act that parrot one of the opening questions in this chapter: Why is the public sector involved in technology transfer? As stated by Congress in the above quoted passage from the Act, during a period of national concern about the widespread productivity slowdown in many sectors of the economy:

> The Federal laboratories and other performers of federally funded research and development frequently provide scientific and technological developments of potential use to State and local governments and private industry [and the developments] should be made accessible to ... improve the economic, environmental, and social well-being of the United States ...

Should the public sector have guidance on such technology transfer activities? The answer is, Yes.

The IAWGTT

As background, the origin of the Interagency Workgroup on Technology Transfer—or Interagency Working Group on Technology Transfer as it is often called—(IAWGTT) traces to President Ronald Reagan's April 10, 1987, Executive Order 12591, Facilitating Access to Science and Technology:

(a)   Within 1 year from the date of this Order, the Director of the Office of Science and Technology Policy[13] shall convene an interagency task force, comprised of the heads of representative agencies and the directors of representative Federal laboratories, or their designees, in order to identify and disseminate creative approaches to technology transfer from Federal laboratories. The task force will report to the President on the progress of and problems with technology transfer from Federal laboratories.

(b)   Specifically, the report shall include:
   (1)   a listing of current technology transfer programs and an assessment of the effectiveness of these programs;
   (2)   identification of new or creative approaches to technology transfer that might serve as model programs for Federal laboratories;
   (3)   criteria to assess the effectiveness and impact on the Nation's economy of planned or future technology transfer efforts; and
   (4)   a compilation and assessment of the Technology Share Program established in Section 2 and, where appropriate, related cooperative research and development venture programs.

This Executive Order applied across all of the appropriate federal agencies. Since 1987, the then Office of Technology Policy within the Technology Administration of the DOC submitted to Congress biannual reports as required by the Federal Technology Transfer Act of 1986:

> Two years after the date of the enactment of this subsection and every two years thereafter, the Secretary shall submit a summary report to the President and the Congress on the use by the agencies and the Secretary of the authorities specified in this Act.

Currently, these annual reports are prepared and submitted to the President and the Congress through the Technology Partnerships Office at NIST.[14] The source for the Technology Partnerships Office's composite report consists of annual reports from each agency. Specifically, under the Technology Transfer Commercialization Act of 2000 (Public Law 106–404):

> Each Federal agency ... shall report annually to the Office of Management and Budget ... on the activities performed by that agency and its Federal laboratories ... The report shall include ... an explanation of the agency's technology transfer program for the preceding fiscal year and the agency's plans for conducting its technology transfer function ... [I]nformation on technology transfer activities for the preceding fiscal year [shall include] (i) the number of patent applications filed; (ii) the number of patents received; (iii) the number of fully-executed licenses which received royalty income in the preceding fiscal year ... (iv) the total earned royalty income ... [and] (vii) any other parameters or discussion that the agency deems relevant or unique to its practice of technology transfer.

The IAWGTT is comprised of technology transfer representatives from each involved agency. Its purpose is to discuss best practices in technology transfer from federal agencies. It is coordinated by the director of the Technology Partnerships Office at NIST.

Table 1.1 chronicles the technology transfer legislation that followed the Stevenson-Wydler Act of 1980 primarily into the 1990s; however, the research activities of U.S. federal laboratories and their technology transfer activities again took centerstage during the early recovery period following the Great Recession (December 2007–June 2009).[15]

President Barack Obama's 2011 Presidential Memorandum

In October, 2011, President Barack Obama issued his Presidential Memorandum—Accelerating Technology Transfer and Commercialization of Federal Research in Support of High-Growth Businesses. The purpose of President Obama's memorandum was to emphasize, as the economy was growing again after the Great Recession, the relationship among technology transfer, innovation, and economic growth. This point merits a restatement:

> Innovation fuels economic growth, the creation of new industries, companies, jobs, products and services, and the global competitiveness of U.S. industries. One driver of successful innovation is technology transfer, in which the private sector adapts Federal research for use in the marketplace ... I direct that [federal laboratories] establish goals and measure performance, streamline administrative processes, and facilitate local and regional partnerships in order to accelerate technology transfer and support private sector commercialization.

In November 2012, IAWGTT issued a response to the President's October 2011 Memorandum (IAWGTT, 2012). Its response specifically mentioned the need for a more detailed reporting of CRADAs (as discussed in Chapter 5) activity, by agency, especially with regard to such partnerships with small businesses. The response stated (p. 7): "new metrics will be included to demonstrate and encourage collaboration with small businesses."

Although not a formal technology transfer policy, President Donald Trump's Administration also raised important issues about technology transfer from federal laboratories. In the President's Management Agenda (PMA, undated), the Administration noted (p. 49):

> The Federal Government invests approximately $150 billion annually in research and development (R&D) conducted at Federal laboratories, universities, and other research organizations. For America to maintain its position as the leader in global innovation, bring products to market more quickly, grow the economy, and maintain a strong national security innovation base, it is essential to optimize technology transfer and support programs to increase the return on investment (ROI) from federally funded R&D.

To re-emphasize, under the heading of a Cross Agency Priority (CAP) Goal to Improve Transfer of Federally Funded Technologies from Lab to Market in the President's Management Agenda (p. 49), the Administration seeks to:

> Improve the transfer of technology from federally funded research and development to the private sector to promote U.S. economic growth and national security.

More specifically, this CAP Goal will (p. 49):

- Improve the transition of federally funded innovations from the laboratory to the marketplace by reducing the administrative and regulatory burdens for technology transfer and increasing private sector investment in later-stage R&D;
- Develop and implement more effective partnering models and technology transfer mechanisms for Federal agencies; and
- Enhance the effectiveness of technology transfer by improving the methods for evaluating the ROI and economic and national security impacts of federally funded R&D, and using that information to focus efforts on approaches proven to work.

The Trump Administration set forth a five-point strategy to accomplish this goal (p. 49):

Agencies will focus on five strategies:
(1) identify regulatory impediments and administrative improvements in Federal technology transfer policies and practices;
(2) increase engagement with private sector technology development experts and investors;
(3) build a more entrepreneurial R&D workforce;
(4) support innovative tools and services for technology transfer; and
(5) improve understanding of global science and technology trends and benchmarks.

In April 2019, NIST released a report titled: "Return on Investment Initiative for Unleashing American Innovation." This report is also known as "The Green Paper." The report articulated the intent of the President's Management Agenda goal to improve the transfer of federally R&D funded technologies from lab to market in a cogent manner (NIST, 2019, pp. 1–3):

The Return on Investment (ROI) Initiative for Unleashing American Innovation is part of a national conversation that is designed to advance the Lab-to-Market cross agency priority (CAP) goal of the President's Management Agenda (PMA). The ROI Initiative's vision is to unleash American innovation into our economy. The objective of the Lab-to-Market CAP Goal is to maximize the transfer of Federal investments in science and technology into value for America in ways that will (a) meet current and future economic and national security needs in a rapidly shifting technology marketplace and enhance U.S. competitiveness globally, and (b) attract greater private sector investment to create innovative products, processes, and services, as well as new businesses and industries … The United States (U.S.) has led the world in innovation, research, and technology development since World War II, but that leadership is being challenged on a global scale. At risk is America's leadership in industries of the future such as artificial intelligence, quantum computing, and robotics. In combination with the rapid, foundational advances in technology, innovation has never been more critical to U.S. economic competitiveness and national security than it is today … The President's Management Agenda (PMA), released March 20, 2018, lays out a long-term vision for modernizing the Federal Government for the 21st Century. The Return on Investment (ROI) Initiative directly supports the PMA and is designed to unleash American innovation. ROI refers here to the economic and national security return to the Nation based on the investment in Federal research and development (R&D) by the American people.

The question about the economic and social impacts of federally funded R&D is certainly not a new question, as was pointed out above, although it remains an important question, as emphasized by the Trump Administration. In 2011, the Committee on Measuring Economics and Other Returns on Federal Research Investments, and the Committee on Science, Engineering, and Public Policy, both within the National Research Council of the National Academies, held a workshop on this topic. The summary of the workshop began with the following statement to emphasize what was at the time an almost decade-old policy question (National Research Council, 2011, p. 1):

> The enactment of the America COMPETES Act in 2006 (and its reauthorization in 2010), the increase in research expenditures under the 2009 American Recovery and Reinvestment Act (ARRA), and President Obama's general emphasis on the contribution of science and technology to economic growth have all heightened interest in the role of scientific and engineering research in creating jobs, generating innovative technologies, spawning new industries, improving health, and producing other economic and societal benefits. Along with this interest has come a renewed emphasis on a question that has been asked for decades: *Can the impacts and practical benefits of research to society be measured either quantitatively or qualitatively?* [emphasis added]

One of the overarching conclusions from the workshop was that academic work has made progress on measuring dimensions of the social impact of federal investments in research[16] especially in the areas related to research funded by the NIH. But "more research is needed on the effects of other funding agencies" (National Research Council, 2011, p. 173). And some might interpret the ROI initiative by the Trump Administration as calling for just that—broader focused research aimed at federal laboratories.

To come full circle, as a means of relating the previous discussion about the early actions of Congress to the theme of this book, the Congressional Research Service (CRS) reported about the 117th Congress, which was convened on January 3, 2021 and will end on January 3, 2023 (CRS, 2021, p. 5):

> Congress is broadly interested in promoting the transfer of technology to address societal needs, promote economic growth, and enhance national welfare and security. Technology transfer from federal laboratories can occur in many forms. In some instances, it can occur through formal partnerships and joint research activities between federal laboratories and private firms, including through cooperative research and development agreements. In other cases, it can occur when the federal government licenses its patent rights to a private firm.

ORGANIZATION OF THE BOOK

The remainder of this book is organized as follows.[17] Chapter 2 is based on the established premise that technology transfer mechanisms used by the public sector are a subset of broader knowledge transfer mechanisms. In 2020, the European Commission (EC) released a report on knowledge transfer metrics and the importance of these metrics to publicly funded research organizations (PROs). The argument set forth by the EC is that "knowledge transfers are an essential source of innovation" (European Commission, 2020, p. 6). This chapter expands on that argument, and it posits that traditional technology transfer mechanisms are a subset of knowledge transfer mechanisms and thus they have a similar impact on innovation and economic growth as do knowledge transfers. Examples of both knowledge transfer and technology transfer mechanisms are discussed in a comparative light.

Absent from the literature on technology transfer activities and related mechanisms is a detailed history of the origin of the *concept* of technology transfer. While some contextual history of technology transfer is presented above, Chapter 3 places U.S. technology transfer activities and mechanisms in an historical context beginning with the actions and activities of the American colonists ... if not even earlier. To illustrate statistically how the concept of technology transfer has evolved over time, the research emphasis on the topic of technology transfer is traced over a period of almost two decades using a keyword analysis based on information from the abstracts of published papers in the *Journal of Technology Transfer*.

Chapter 4 presents a detailed history of the FLC, which is mentioned above, since being founded in the early 1970s. This chapter provides the context for how federal laboratories operationalized technology transfer legislation beginning with the Stevenson-Wydler Act of 1980. This chapter also places the FLC in the position of being a unique as well as an important organization or infrastructure that supports the technology-based economic growth of the Nation.

Chapter 5 presents a descriptive and statistical analysis of federal laboratory technology transfer mechanisms and metrics for each of the 11 major federal agencies. The statistical analysis is motivated by an allocation model that associates federal basic research and applied research allocations (i.e., financial inputs) with various knowledge transfer and technology transfer mechanisms (i.e., technical outputs). The data used in Chapter 5 come from published and unpublished reports by the Technology Partnerships Office within NIST and the American Association for the Advancement of Science (AAAS).

Not all federally funded technologies emanate from the research conducted in federal laboratories or even from research funded by the laboratory's host agencies. However, yet to be systematically described or statistically evaluated in the academic and policy literatures are systematic studies of technologies from federally funded research that occur in small firms.[18] In Chapter 6, the SBIR program and STTR program are discussed from an institutional perspective.[19]

Not only is technology transferred from federal agency funded firms into society, but also others' technologies are also transferred into federal agency funded firms. Building on the institutional foundation in Chapter 6, and on data from the National Research Council on SBIR and STTR research projects, Chapter 7 considers the extent to which SBIR and STTR funded firms transfer knowledge and technology to others through mechanisms similar to those discussed in Chapter 5.

Chapter 8 introduces a previously unexplored dimension of federally funded technology that is transferred to other firms. This mechanism is the sale of rights to technology developed by SBIR and STTR funded research to other U.S. firms. The empirical findings in this chapter show that such transfers are more likely to occur in smaller rather than larger firms.

Chapter 9 extends the discussion of SBIR funded technology transfers. Specifically, technology transfers from so-called *SBIR mills* are documented in light of discussions related to the recent reauthorization of the SBIR program through the SBIR and STTR Extension Act of 2022.

In the concluding Chapter 10, the information from the previous chapters is summarized and, building on that information, a research agenda is suggested for future studies of public sector technology transfer in the United States as well as in other countries.

NOTES

1.   In more detail, the eight categories of risk and uncertainty that the private sector firm faces when making investments in R&D are (Link and Scott, 2011):

   •   High technical risk associated with the underlying R&D: the risk of the R&D project is greater than what the firm can accept, although if the R&D is successful there would be large benefits to society as a whole.

   •   High capital costs to undertake the underlying R&D: the R&D project may require too much financial and human capital for any one firm to expend, and thus the firm will not invest in the R&D project although society would be better off if it did.

   •   Long time to complete the R&D project and commercialize the resulting technology: the time expected to complete the R&D project and the time until commercialization of the R&D results are both long and variable, and thus a cash flow issue may overwhelm the firm and deter third-party investors.

   •   Underlying R&D spills over to multiple markets and is not appropriable: it is not uncommon for the scope of potential markets for the technology that results from the R&D project to be broader than the scope of the individual firm's market strategies. Thus, the firm will not perceive or project economic benefits from all potential market applications of the technology and thus the firm will underestimate the potential returns it can earn compared to the cost of the R&D project.

   •   Market success of the technology depends on technologies in different industries: markets evolve over time and thus R&D investments in a portfolio of projects might be needed, but pursuit of such a portfolio might be beyond the financial and technical capabilities of the firm.

   •   Property rights cannot be assigned to the underlying R&D: not all property rights from any technology that results from the R&D project can be appropriated by the firm, and thus they might spill over to other firm,s especially competing firms.

   •   Resulting technology must be compatible and interoperable with other technologies: technology-based products are often part of larger systems of products, and that system might not exist or might not be mature when the initial R&D investment is made, hence there is a risk that the resulting technology might not be able to interface with other products in the market.

- High risk of opportunistic behavior when sharing information about the technology: there are situations that exist where the complexity of the R&D resulting technology requires an agreement on expected product performance between potential buyers and the firm, and such agreements have elements of uncertainty and thus are costly.

2. Research knowledge is knowledge of a particular kind especially when compared to the definition of knowledge by Carrillo (2022, p. 8): "Knowledge is a night cat. Familiar, yet enigmatic. Ubiquitous, yet furtive."

3. See Samuelson (1954) for a discussion of public goods.

4. The concept of market failure traces to the writings of the English philosopher Henry Sidgwick (1838–1900) (Medema, 2007), although the concept was introduced into contemporary economics by Bator (1958).

5. As Link and Wagner (2021, p. 761) noted, the term *Founding Fathers* refers to "that generation of men who were active in the American Revolution and the formation of the early American Republic and the Constitution." See https://oll.libertyfund.org/group/the-founding-fathers-of-the-u-s-constitution, accessed November 26, 2022.

6. See also Eisenberg (1996, p. 1671) who wrote: "The question of who should own title to [government-sponsored] research results has been the subject of heated debate at least since World War II, when unprecedented levels of federal spending on research and development to support the war effort focused the attention of the federal government on the issue."

7. I might add to this quotation the following: "… so that authors and inventors can profit from their science and useful arts and thus later have an incentive to transfer their applied knowledge to others."

8. See the discussion about these debates by Brooks (1996) and Link (2022b).

9. The material that follows in this section relates to contemporary technology transfer legislation. In fact, many will point to the Stevenson-Wydler Act of 1980 and the Bayh-Dole Act of 1980 as the foundational technology transfer legislation. In Chapter 3, I will discuss antecedent activity and legislation to these Acts. See also Latker's (2000) discussion about intellectual property at the NIH.

10. See https://www.loc.gov/item/fr010116/. There were amendments to this executive order: https://www.archives.gov/federalregister/executive-orders/1945-truman.html. Both sources were accessed on December 3, 2022.

11. For a discussion about other U.S. legislation, see Link and Cunningham (2021) and Link and Van Hasselt (2023). Specifically, the Bayh-Dole Act of 1980 (formally, the University and Small Business Patent Protection Act of 1980) redefined property rights to facilitate the transfer of existing knowledge resulting from public sector funded research in universities to the private sector; the R&E (Research and Experimentation) Tax Credit portion of the Economic Recovery Tax Act of 1981 provided a marginal tax credit to private sector firms on qualified R&E expenditures in excess of the average amount spent during the previous three taxable years; and the National Cooperative Research Act of 1984 created a registration process under which joint R&D ventures can voluntarily disclose their research intension to the U.S. Department of Justice and thereby gain partial indemnification from antitrust laws and penalties. The Small Business Innovation Development Act of 1982 is discussed in Chapter 6.

12. One might also interpret "to State and local governments" in the last sentence of the quotation to suggest that there is a failure in those units of government to invest in technology-based resources to a social level.
13. The Office of Science and Technology Policy (OSTP), created in 1976, is a department within the Executive Office of the President. See Hart (2014) for an historical overview of the OSTP.
14. See https://www.nist.gov/tpo, accessed December 3, 2022.
15. The following discussion about the emphasis on technology transfer by the Obama Administration and the Trump Administration draws directly from Link and Oliver (2020).
16. See Link and Van Hasselt (2023).
17. Several of the topics about technology transfer in this book are extensions of material from Link and Oliver (2020).
18. Link and Van Hasselt (2023) is also an effort in this direction.
19. I, along with my colleagues, have written about the SBIR program and the STTR program many times. As a result, duplication of text, and especially legislative information in Chapter 6, from previous writings is inevitable.

2. Knowledge transfers and technology transfers

INTRODUCTION

The purpose of this book is to provide analytical information to characterize U.S. public sector knowledge and technology transfer activities, and to enhance that purpose it is important to first place public sector knowledge transfers and technology transfers under the umbrella of a public response to market failure. An understanding of the sources of knowledge is a reasonable and useful starting point not only to give context to fulfilling this goal but also to segue to a more detailed study of technology transfers.

SOURCES OF KNOWLEDGE

Perhaps there is no better place to begin a discussion about sources of knowledge than with an overview of the thoughts and ideas about the subject as penned by John Locke.[1]

Locke was born in 1632 in the hamlet of Wrighton, in the county of Somerset, in southwest England. Educated with a B.A. and M.A. at Oxford University, and trained in medicine at that same institution, Locke soon transcended his formal training to become one of the most influential philosophers of his time, posthumously receiving the titles of Founder of British Empiricism and Father of Classical Liberalism.

Arguably, Locke's most famous treatise is *An Essay Concerning Human Understanding*, first published in 1689 (but dated as 1690). Locke elaborated on many themes in *Essay*, several of which are fundamental to setting the stage for the discussion about sources of knowledge as antecedents of knowledge transfers and technology transfers, and thus of economic growth.

Locke began his essay with an exploration of the genesis of ideas.[2] He emphasized that all ideas emanate from sensation or reflection (Locke, 1996, p. 33):

> Every man being conscious to himself, that he thinks, and that which his mind is employed about whilst thinking being the *ideas*, that are there, 'tis past doubt, that

men have in their minds several *ideas … All ideas come from sensation or reflection.* [original emphasis]

Regarding sensation, Locke emphasized one's perception of things, and perception is fundamental to understanding one's behavior (Locke, 1996, pp. 33–4):

> *[O]ur senses*, conversant about particular sensible objects, do *convey into the mind* several distinct *perceptions* of things, according to those various ways, wherein those objects do affect them: and thus we come by those *ideas* we have of *yellow, white, heat, cold, soft, hard, bitter, sweet,* and all those which we call sensible qualities, which when I say the senses convey into the mind, I mean, they from external objects convey into the mind what produces there those *perceptions.* This great source, of most of the *ideas* we have, depending wholly upon our senses, and derived by them to the understanding, I call *SENSATION.* [original emphasis]

As an aside, Hébert and Link (2009, p. 105) argued that perception is the genesis of entrepreneurial action:

> … we rely on the most elemental features of entrepreneurship—perception, courage, and action … Entrepreneurial action means creation of opportunity as well as response to existing circumstances. Entrepreneurial action also implies that entrepreneurs have the courage to embrace risks in the face of uncertainty. The failure of perception, nerve, or action renders the entrepreneur ineffective. For this reason, we must look to these elements for the distinctive nature of the concept, not to the circumstances of action or reaction.

Locke did not write about entrepreneurship, and his view of perception being the antecedent of action was only to conceptualizing perception leading to an individual having ideas.

And regarding reflection, Locke, perhaps being influenced by his Puritanical upbringing and his continued search for an understanding of God, acknowledged that one's soul or internal senses temper one's perceptions (Locke, 1996, p. 34):

> [T]he other fountain, from which experience furnishes the understanding with *ideas* is the *perception of the operations of our own minds* within us, as it is employed about the *ideas* it has got; which operations, when the soul comes to reflect on, and consider, do furnish the understanding with another set of *ideas,* which could not be had from things without: and such are, *perception, thinking, doubting, believing, reasoning, knowing, willing,* and all the different actings of our own minds; which we being conscious of, and observing in ourselves, do from these receive into our understandings, as distinct *ideas,* as we do from bodies affecting our senses. This source of *ideas,* every man has wholly in himself: and though it be not sense, as having nothing to do with external objects; yet it is very like it, and might properly enough be called internal sense. But as I call the other *sensation,* so I call this

REFLECTION, the *ideas* it affords being such only, as the mind gets by reflecting on its own operations within itself. [original emphasis]

But, as clear as Locke was about sensation and reflection being the "fountains of knowledge" (1996, p. 33) from which ideas spring, he was also clear that one's mind is not a blank slate. There is a precursor to one's knowledge, and that precursor is one's experiences. More eloquently, Locke wrote (1996, p. 33):

> Let us then suppose the mind to be, as we say, white paper, void of all characters, without any *ideas*; how comes it to be furnished? Whence comes it by that vast store, which the busy and boundless fancy of man has painted on it, with an almost endless variety? Whence has it all the materials of reason and knowledge? To this I answer, in one word, from *experience*; in that, all our knowledge is founded; and from that it ultimately derives itself. Our observation employed either, about *external sensible objects* [i.e., sensations], *or about the internal operations of our minds, perceived and reflected on by ourselves* [i.e., reflection], *is that, which supplies our understandings with all the materials of thinking.* These two are the fountains of knowledge, from whence all the *ideas* we have, or can naturally have, do spring. [original emphasis]

KNOWLEDGE TRANSFERS AND TECHNOLOGY TRANSFERS

The European Commission (2020, p. 8) recently addressed the topic of knowledge transfer (KT):

> KT is about getting research and expertise put to use which, by its nature is wide-ranging and complex.

Research, as emphasized in the above quoted excerpt, has two broad output categories: new knowledge and improved researchers.[3] One might broadly think of these two output categories as technical knowledge and human capital or experiential knowledge, respectively, or perhaps as codified knowledge and tacit knowledge, respectively.

As an output, new knowledge can be embodied in publications, processes, materials, and technology. Researchers benefit from being engaged in the research process through know-how, innovativeness, and new skills. Relevant questions, and these questions have policy overtones, are: How do one's experiences reveal themselves in the form of new knowledge outputs? and How do the experiences embodied within researchers enrich economic growth and thus society?

Locke talked about an individual's experiences being the source of new knowledge, and he envisioned these experiences being born first hand through reflections. However, new knowledge can come to an individual through the experiences of or sensations from others that are shared through access to the outputs of research: publications, processes, materials, technology, know-how, innovativeness, and skills. In other words, one individual's experiences, gleaned through reflections, can be manifested in new knowledge and those experiences then become sensations for another individual.

The channels through which experiences are passed include (in the same order of occurrence as presented in European Commission, 2020): publications and presentations, teaching, networking/events, consultancy, professional development, collaborative research, contract research, licensing, and company creation.

From a U.S. perspective, the so-called mirepoix of technology transfer channels or mechanisms are patents, licenses, and collaborative research efforts (NIST, 2022); however, the Technology Partnerships Office at NIST noted within the context of technology transfer that (NIST, 2022, p. 12):[4]

> ... most federal research results are transferred through publication of S&E [science and engineering] articles.

Thus, three of the nine European Commission knowledge channels mentioned above—publications, collaborative research, and licensing—are referred to, at least by the National Institute of Standards and Technology (NIST), as technology transfer mechanisms.

I think that one could infer from differences in the European Commission's knowledge taxonomy and NIST's technology taxonomy that there is an intertwined relationship over time between knowledge transfer channels and technology transfer mechanisms.

EXAMPLES OF KNOWLEDGE TRANSFERS AND TECHNOLOGY TRANSFERS

Three examples of knowledge and technology transfers are discussed in this section although the mechanisms of patents, licenses, and collaborations are discussed again in detail in Chapter 5. The first two examples deal with metrology, the study of measurement science, and its related research outputs that come from NIST. The third example deals with science and engineering (S&E) publications by scientists across federal agencies.

The following first two examples are specialized and likely are not familiar to most readers, but the attendant discussion below shows their quantitative importance to aggregate economic growth. Selected econometric findings are presented here to emphasize the statistical strength of the relationship between the transfer mechanisms and economic growth, but the interested reader should see the cited literature for a more detailed discussion of all of the econometric results. These two examples fall broadly under the transfer heading of public information, as does the content of S&E publications. NIST is emphasized in these first two examples because it is the national metrology institute of the United States.[5]

Calibration testing is a for-fee service that allows for public information to be used for specific purposes. Standard Reference Materials (SRMs) are also an example of public information being used for specific purposes. Based on extensive interviews with companies that are involved in both calibration testing at NIST as well as the purchase of SRMs from NIST, I have come to the conclusion that the use of calibration testing is part of a firm's defensive strategy to maintain market share and to generate new sales. Thus, my perception is that at the aggregate level the use of calibration testing is associated with aggregate economic growth. In contrast, I also have come to the conclusion that firms use SRMs in a response to changes in economic conditions. Thus, my perception is that at the aggregate level changes in economic conditions bring about a greater use of SRMs. The empirical analyses to date (e.g., Hall et al., 2022; Link, 2021) related to these forms of knowledge spillovers are insufficient to support systematically and empirically my interview-based perceptions about firms' strategic use of SRMs, but the analyses presented below are not necessarily inconsistent with my conclusions.

The third example is S&E publications across agencies. S&E publications allow for public information to become a foundation for future scientific inquiries by authors and others and, with reflection of Locke's writings, to provide second-hand experiences to others in their quest for new ideas.

Calibration Tests[6]

Calibration tests are a mechanism through which NIST's advancements in metrology are transferred to private and public sector organizations to ensure standardized measurements. According to NIST (USDOC, 2019, p. 24), calibration tests are explained in the following way:

> The NIST laboratories provide unique physical measurement services for their customers, including calibration services, special tests, and measurement assurance programs. NIST designs its calibration services to help manufacturers and users of precision instruments achieve the highest possible levels of measurement quality and productivity. NIST calibrations often serve as the basis for companies that provide commercial calibration services and calibration equipment.

From a theoretical perspective, Swann (2009, p. 60) pointed out, and Link (2022a) discussed in more detail, that standardized measurements reduce transaction costs between buyers and sellers:

> The accurate measurement of product characteristics makes it easier to demonstrate quality and safety, and hence to sustain a price premium for superior products. Because of this, measurement also plays an important role in the reduction of market failure.[7]

Table 2.1 shows the number of calibration tests performed at NIST, by fiscal year (FY). The data in the table suggest that calibration tests decreased during the Great Recession (December 2007–June 2009), and usage has not recovered.

Table 2.1   *Calibration tests performed at NIST by fiscal year*
                   FY1999–FY2018

Fiscal Year (FY)	Number of Calibration Tests
1999	3,118
2000	2,969
2001	3,192
2002	2,924
2003	13,987
2004	12,503
2005	12,849
2006	13,127
2007	27,489
2008	25,944
2009	18,609
2010	17,697
2011	18,195
2012	17,206
2013	14,974
2014	15,401
2015	13,906
2016	12,971
2017	13,802
2018	11,771

Source: https://www.nist.gov/tpo/department-commerce, accessed December 20, 2022.

Many of the empirical illustrations that follow focus on the Great Recession in the United States under the umbrella of an event study. My focus on the Great Recession is motivated by the likelihood that lessons learned from a comparison of pre- and post-recession activities might be a bellwether for policy makers.

Many of the empirical illustrations in the following chapters focus on the Great Recession in the United States. First, in a narrow but important sense, understanding the impact of the Great Recession on knowledge and technology transfer activities might illustrate some lessons to be learned, and those lessons might be informative for policy decisions.[8] Second, in a broader and equally important sense, one might think of comparing technology transfers in the pre-Great Recession to the post-Great Recession as an event case study related to how public sector entrepreneurs—a concept discussed and illustrated in Chapter 3—react to a disequilibrium (i.e., Great Recession) situation.

Anticipating the discussion in Chapter 3, public sector entrepreneurship is defined by Leyden and Link (2015, p. 14) as:

> [P]ublic sector entrepreneurship refers to innovative public policy initiatives that generate greater economic prosperity by transforming a status quo economic environment into one that is more conducive to economic units engaging in creative activities in the face of uncertainty.

And Leyden and Link make the case that a public sector entrepreneur might be a person or an organization in the public sector. The actions of such a person or organization might result in a policy that "transforms a status quo economic environment."

There is a literature in economics and management that has focused on the creative response of *firms* to the Great Recession (e.g., Archibugi et al., 2013; Donald et al., 2013). Many of these authors couch their empirical studies in the context of a Schumpeterian-like response by the private sector creative economy to economic events. I am not convinced that the public sector's response to the Great Recession through knowledge and technology transfers, which is without question a creative activity, parallels how a Schumpeterian private sector firm responds to a disequilibrium situation. In the vein of searching for a public sector context to support a pre-Great Recession versus post-Great Recession comparison, I suggest that one consider the arguments not of Schumpeter but rather of Shackle and Schultz. Although each of these two eminent scholars looked at entrepreneurship and entrepreneurial activity from the perspective of individuals in the private sector rather than public sector, a coupling of uncertainty and creativity is, I believe, relevant, or perhaps even a motivation, to explore technology transfer activities in a pre- and post-Great Recession environment.

Shackle (1966) identified two roles that must be performed by an enterprise which I am embellishing to refer to a public sector entrepreneur or public sector organization—the organization considered in this book is a federal agency or its laboratory(ies). One role is bearing uncertainty; the other role is making maximizing decisions in the face of uncertainty. These two roles are related because decision making involves improvisation or invention—actions that are genuinely possible only in a world of uncertainty.

Reflecting on the ideas of Alfred Marshall, time in the world of affairs must also be considered. Time is known to weave an historical tapestry, and each of the threads is the consequences of human decisions. Accordingly, Shackle wrote (Shackle, 1966, p. 73):

> ... we take it for granted that a responsibility lies upon us for our acts; that these acts are in a profound sense creative, inceptive, the source of historical novelty; that each such act is, as it were, the unconnected starting point of a new thread in the tapestry which time is weaving.

Hébert and Link (2009) interpreted this view of Shackle, without public sector entrepreneurial action in mind although herein I am so relating it to that construct, to mean that uncertainty is a subjective state of mind that is bounded by possibility. Only bounded uncertainty, which certainly characterized the Great Recession, will provide a relevant environment to permit a public-sector entrepreneur to act creatively as reflected through the development and transfer of technology.

Hébert and Link (2009) argued that Schultz (1975) contributed to the theoretical identification of an entrepreneur in two ways; he redefined the concept of entrepreneurship as an ability to deal with disequilibria, and he posited and illustrated empirically that human capital (i.e., education) enhances the ability of an entrepreneur to perceive and react to disequilibria.

Thus, to return to the theme of this book, if the Great Recession is viewed as a period of disequilibrium, a comparison of technology transfer activity in the pre- and post-Great Recession might define a federal agency as being entrepreneurial through an increase in its technology transfer efforts. And, if those efforts are guided by the actions of a public sector entrepreneur, his/her educational background might determine, at least in part, the efficiency of his/her technology transfer efforts.

Figure 2.1 shows the trend in calibration tests. The trend is clearly a positive trend until the economy declined during the Great Recession, and the decline has continued past the end of the recession. To estimate empirically the relationship between the number of calibration tests (*CalibrationTests*) and the years of the Great Recession, I considered the following model:

$$CalibrationTests = f\left(Trend, PostRecession\right) \qquad (2.1)$$

where the variable *Trend* equals 1 in FY1999 and *Trend* equals 20 in 2018; the variable *PostRecession* equals 1 for years after 2007, and 0 otherwise; and the variable *TrendPostRecession* is an interaction variable equal to *Trend x PostRecession*. The regression results from the estimation of equation (2.1) are in Table 2.2, and they do document empirically an inverted-V trend.

Table 2.2   *Regression results quantifying the inverted-V trend in calibration tests (n = 20) (p-values in parentheses)*

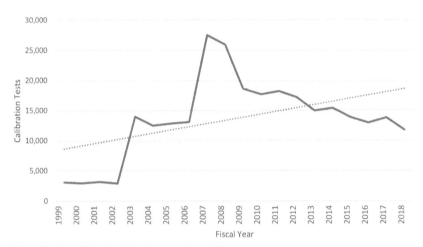

Note: The dotted line is an Excel-generated trend line.

Figure 2.1   *Trend in calibration tests (n = 20), by fiscal year FY1919–FY2018*

Variable	Estimated Coefficient
Trend	2614
	(p < .0001)
TrendPostRecession	−3656
	(p <.0001)
PostRecession	34,873
	(p < .0001
Intercept	−2831
	(p < .0001)
R^2	0.818

In pre-recession years (*PostRecession* = 0), the estimated coefficient on *Trend* is positive (2,614) and significant; in the post-recession years (*PostRecession* = 1), the estimated coefficient on *Trend* is negative (2,614 − 3,656 = −1,042) and significant. In the pre-recession period the number of calibration tests increased by an average of 2,614 per year; in the post-recession period the number of calibration tests decreases by an average of 1,042 per year. Also visible from Figure 2.1, the slope of the trend in *CalibrationTests* is steeper in the pre-recession period than in the post-recession period.

As stated in Chapter 1, knowledge transfers and technology transfers have a positive impact on economic growth. An exploratory econometric analysis of an aspect of the data in Table 2.1 is also presented in Table 2.3. The dependent variable in this model is an index of multifactor productivity (*MFP*).[9] The multifactor productivity index is widely regarded as a measure of technological advancement over time. Held constant in this model is a measure of available R&D resources (*NISTLabR&D*) and a control for the years of the Great Recession (*GreatRecession*). The regression coefficient on *CalibrationTests* suggest that a 10 percent increase in the number of calibration tests performed at NIST is associated with a 0.30 percent increase in the multifactor productivity index relevant to the U.S. private non-farm business sector of the economy.[10]

Table 2.3   *Descriptive data and exploratory regression results, dependent variable is log(MFP) (n = 20) (p-values in parentheses)*

Variable	Definition	Mean	Standard Deviation	Range
MFP	Multifactor productivity index for the U.S. private business sector (2012 = 100) https://www.bls.gov/mfp/tables.htm	96.94	4.58	87.70–102.79
CalibrationTests	Number of calibration tests performed at NIST by fiscal year https://www.nist.gov/tpo/department -commerce	13,631.70	6,796.26	2,924–27,489
NISTLabR&D	NIST laboratory R&D budget ($2,020 million) by fiscal year https://www.aaas.org/programs/r-d -budget-and-policy/historical-trends -federal-rd	577.70	116.60	414.60–753.10
GreatRecession	=1 if FY = 2008, 2009, or 2010; 0 otherwise	0.15	0.37	0/1

Variable	Estimated Coefficient
log(CalibrationTests)	0.030
	(p < .0001)
log(NISTLabR&D)	0.159
	(p < .0001)
GreatRecession	−0.014
	(p < .0001)
Intercept	3.290
	(p < .0001)
R^2	0.957

Standard Reference Materials[11]

Standard Reference Materials:[12]

> ... are used to perform instrument calibrations in units as part of overall quality assurance programs, to verify the accuracy of specific measurements and to support the development of new measurement methods ... An SRM is prepared and used for three main purposes: (1) to help develop accurate methods of analysis; (2) to calibrate measurement systems used to facilitate exchange of goods, institute quality control, determine performance characteristics, or measure a property at the state-of-the-art limit; and (3) to ensure the long-term adequacy and integrity of measurement quality assurance programs.

To provide context for a discussion of SRMs, the National Bureau of Standards (NBS), which became NIST in 1988 through the Omnibus Trade and Competitiveness Act of 1988 (Public Law 100–418),[13] played a pioneering role in the United States in the establishment of SRMs for more than a century. As chronicled by Schooley (2000, p. 110), the Standard Reference Materials program at the NBS traces its response to the American Foundrymen's Association request in 1905:

> ... for help in producing standard samples of cast iron to promote uniform analytical and manufacturing techniques.

But, it was not until 1964 that a formal Office of Standard Reference Materials was established at the NBS (Schooley, 2000, p. 110):[14]

> ... to evaluate the requirements of science and industry for carefully characterized reference materials and to stimulate NBS efforts to create, produce, and distribute such materials.

The Office of Reference Materials (ORM) at NIST currently:[15]

> ... operates and maintains the business information systems to support customer, financial, inventory, project tracking, and sales functions related to both the SRM program and calibration services.

More than 1,300 SRMs are now certified and maintained at NIST.

Hall et al. (2022) provide several examples of SRMs, two of which relate to cholesterol and radiopharmaceuticals.

Cholesterol is a waxy substance found in the blood stream and in cells. Produced in the liver, cholesterol is a key building block for body tissue. NIST currently offers three SRMs related to cholesterol. The economic benefits associated with use of cholesterol SRMs is improved accuracy in patient testing and in reduced variability among laboratories. Reduced variability and improved accuracy in testing lower the transaction costs between producers of test equipment and consumers of test equipment results.

Radiopharmaceuticals are radioactive drugs that target specific organs or tissues in the human body. They are used for diagnostics (e.g., imaging) as well as for therapeutic purposes. NIST produces nine radiopharmaceuticals intended for the calibration of radioactivity-measuring instruments. The economic benefits associated with the use of these SRMs relate to both diagnostic and laboratory research accuracy as well as therapeutics. More accurate diagnoses and laboratory research results in reduced costs, and more accurate and precise treatments are more effective.

The data in Table 2.4 show the number of units of SRMs sold in the United States by fiscal year, FY1988 through FY2019. There is some indication that the sale of SRMs decreased during the Great Recession hitting a low of 13,915 in FY2009, but unlike with calibration tests (see Figure 2.1), the number of units sold quickly rebounded. Figure 2.2 shows the overall trend in SRMs sold. The trend is clearly negative over the entire time period, and the Great Recession dip and recovery is also evident in the figure.

Table 2.4   *SRM units sold in the United States, by fiscal year*
            FY1988–FY2019

Fiscal Year	SRM Units Sold to Customers in the United States
1988	*22,078*
1989	*22,476*
1990	*24,349*
1991	*23,571*
1992	*23,936*
1993	*23,250*
1994	*22,577*
1995	*20,366*
1996	*19,676*
1997	*19,534*
1998	*18,271*
1999	*16,551*
2000	*16,885*
2001	*15,875*
2002	*15,384*
2003	16,208
2004	15,875
2005	16,575
2006	15,559
2007	15,741
2008	16,522
2009	13,915
2010	14,812
2011	15,907
2012	16,791
2013	15,328
2014	16,023
2015	16,654
2016	15,447
2017	16,032
2018	15,360
2019	15,714

Note: The Office of Reference Materials provided Standard Reference Material (SRM) units sold to customers in the United States from FY2003 through FY2019. There was a change in records management in 2003; thus, SRM units sold in the United States prior to that fiscal year were estimated by imputing the mean percentage of SRM units sold in the United States from FY2003 through FY2019 (49.63 percent) to the total SRM units sold from FY1988 through FY2002 (shown in italics).

After the Great Recession, the trend in SRMs sold is above trend. From the estimation of a trend model, the estimated slope coefficient is −245.52 (p <

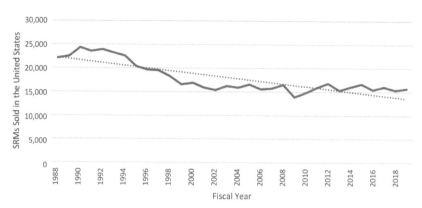

Note: The dotted line is an Excel-generated trend line.

Figure 2.2   *Trend in Standard Reference Materials sold in the United States (n = 32), by fiscal year FY1988–FY2018*

.001) with $R^2 = 0.899$. Over the 32-year period, the number of SRMs sold in the United States decreased on average by 245.5 per year.

S&E Publications

Table 2.5 shows the whole and fractional number of S&E published articles by federal agency and by calendar year.[16] Available data are not sufficient to generalize about the impact of the Great Recession on article counts, but a visual inspection of the data shows that in some agencies the trend over available years of data is increasing and, in some agencies, it is decreasing. Using aggregated data across all federal agencies, the trend in the number of whole count S&E articles is shown in Figure 2.3, and the trend is upward sloping implying that knowledge transfers through publications have generally increased since 2012.

Table 2.5   U.S. science and engineering (S&E) articles, by federal agency, by calendar year 2012–21

Articles on a Whole Count Basis

CY	USDA	DOC	DOD	DOE	HHS	DHS	DOI	DOT	VA	EPA	NASA
2012	6,797	4,321	10,565	18,768	14,903	131	2,708	265	10,333	985	6,395
2013	6,621	4,519	9,868	18,741	14,449	161	2,793	242	10,753	981	6,259
2014	6,588	4,491	9,733	18,614	14,498	119	2,834	240	11,105	960	6,019
2015	6,621	4,378	10,089	18,708	14,569	118	2,796	225	11,265	928	6,003
2016	6,696	4,758	10,201	19,241	14,430	172	2,976	235	11,377	1,032	6,879
2017	7,090	4,738	10,138	19,225	14,407	165	2,891	225	11,489	930	6,410
2018	6,982	4,697	10,306	20,087	14,481	145	2,924	275	11,638	932	7,000
2019	6,969	4,528	10,274	19,332	13,960	129	2,772	207	11,546	816	6,677
2020	6,837	4,537	9,736	19,913	14,179	158	2,871	168	12,422	719	6,591
2021	7,331	4,268	9,099	19,224	15,704	145	3,073	167	14,606	784	5,694

Articles on a Fractional Count Basis (rounded)

CY	USDA	DOC	DOD	DOE	HHS	DHS	DOI	DOT	VA	EPA	NASA
2012	3,259	2,074	5,732	9,432	7,283	61	1,212	130	3,287	487.0	2,864
2013	3,099	2,126	5,145	9,154	6,944	79	1,237	124	3,274	486.1	2,703
2014	2,904	2,070	5,156	8,899	6,852	53	1,254	115	3,267	457.6	2,534
2015	2,855	1,984	5,430	8,779	6,733	55.9	1,185	116	3,222	455.5	2,445
2016	2,828	2,060	5,393	8,747	6,613	88.2	1,261	112	3,173	495.2	2,762
2017	2,952	2,067	5,345	8,655	6,530	65.2	1,206	110	3,156	440.7	2,439
2018	2,844	1,964	5,291	8,880	6,431	59.4	1,195	120	3,114	438.6	2,760
2019	2,753	1,897	5,196	8,394	6,157	52.4	1,130	86	2,961	382.1	2,635
2020	2,661	1,784	4,787	8,575	6,217	70.7	1,173	69	3,098	337.2	2,424
2021	2,673	1,590	4,233	8,141	6,841	56.9	1,197	78	3,570	369.9	1,890

Note: USDA is U.S. Department of Agriculture, DOC is Department of Commerce, DOD is Department of Defense, DOE is Department of Energy, HHS is Department of Health and Human Services, DHS is Department of Homeland Security, DOI is Department of the Interior, DOT is Department of Transportation, VA is Department of Veterans Affairs, EPA is Environmental Protection Agency, NASA is National Aeronautics and Space Administration. Data are presented by calendar year as months of publication are not always available in Scopus. When authors are from more than one federal agency, whole counting gives each agency full credit for the same publication. When authors are from more than one federal agency, fractional counting assigns a portion or fraction of a publication to each agency. Thus, whole counts are not less than fractional counts.
Source: Provided by the Technology Partnerships Office at NIST.

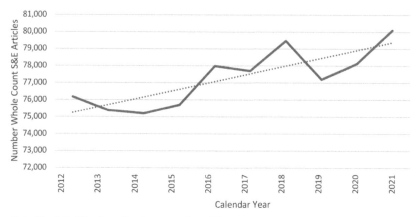

Note: The dotted line is an Excel-generated trend line.

Figure 2.3   *Trend in the number of whole count U.S. science and engineering (S&E) articles for all agencies, by calendar year 2012–21*

The data in Table 2.5 can be combined with U.S. patent data from which a metric of citations to S&E articles in U.S. Patent and Trademark Office (USPTO) patents can be constructed for each federal agency (Table 2.6). Again, using aggregated data across all federal agencies, the trend in these citations are shown in Figure 2.4, and it is upward sloping. The Technology Partnerships Office within NIST refers to the number of articles cited in U.S. patents as evidence of the "commercial relevance of S&E articles authored by federal researchers" (NIST, 2022, p. 13).

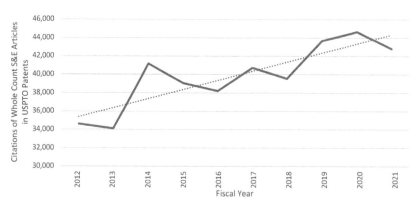

Note: The dotted line is an Excel-generated trend line.

Figure 2.4   *Trend in the citations of whole count U.S. science and engineering (S&E) articles in U.S. Patent and Trademark Office (USPTO) patents for all federal agencies, by fiscal year FY2012–FY2021*

Table 2.6 Citation of U.S. science and engineering (S&E) articles in U.S. Patent and Trademark Office (USPTO) patents, by federal agency and by fiscal year FY2012–FY2021

Articles on a Whole Count Basis

FY	USDA	DOC	DOD	DOE	HHS	DHS	DOI	DOT	VA	EPA	NASA
2012	1,970	1,016	5,114	7,487	12,974	64	78	24	5,507	118	1,887
2013	2,090	1,103	4,932	8,007	11,881	60	97	32	5,820	123	1,672
2014	2,576	1,309	5,816	9,725	14,580	58	80	30	7,157	108	1,716
2015	2,136	1,214	5,151	9,801	14,210	53	93	14	6,369	133	1,638
2016	2,270	1,204	5,274	9,599	13,620	46	101	18	6,172	127	1,498
2017	2,296	1,431	5,237	10,384	14,902	32	142	29	6,855	93	1,308
2018	2,160	1,332	4,944	10,193	14,421	44	191	33	6,759	92	1,410
2019	2,293	1,439	5,401	12,088	15,814	35	177	27	7,263	136	1,359
2020	2,420	1,516	4,999	12,546	16,884	29	194	28	6,990	153	1,357
2021	2,231	1,610	4,725	11,248	16,851	62	163	26	6,863	171	1,216

Articles on a Fractional Count Basis (rounded)

FY	USDA	DOC	DOD	DOE	HHS	DHS	DOI	DOT	VA	EPA	NASA
2012	987	588	2,858	4,212	7,461	28	34	9	1,982	78	1,127
2013	1,072	627	2,727	4,479	6,576	34	51	10	2,034	68	975
2014	1,287	761	3,181	5,463	8,023	27	45	12	2,413	55	991
2015	1,041	689	2,768	5,380	7,607	27	39	4	2,102	72	922
2016	1,113	689	2,789	5,265	7,216	18	40	8	1,998	61	801
2017	1,079	799	2,672	5,299	7,523	11	47	16	2,055	47	677
2018	988	735	2,400	5,047	7,039	16	50	16	1,905	53	692
2019	977	743	2,526	5,700	7,591	16	47	12	1,964	65	670
2020	975	770	2,280	5,676	8,151	10	65	15	1,693	66	649
2021	921	795	2,179	4,877	8,186	29	54	14	1,625	78	604

Note: USDA is U.S. Department of Agriculture, DOC is Department of Commerce, DOD is Department of Defense, DOE is Department of Energy, HHS is Department of Health and Human Services, DHS is Department of Homeland Security, DOI is Department of the Interior, DOT is Department of Transportation, VA is Department of Veterans Affairs, EPA is Environmental Protection Agency, NASA is National Aeronautics and Space Administration.

Data are presented by fiscal year (a fiscal year starts on October 1 of the previous year to September 30 of the current year). When authors are from more than one federal agency, whole counting gives each agency full credit for the same publication. When authors are from more than one federal agency, fractional counting assigns a portion or fraction of a publication to each agency. Thus, whole counts are not less than fractional counts.

Source: Provided by the Technology Partnerships Office at NIST.

Defining *Technology Transfer*

Table 2.7 contains statements that might be informative in defining the term *technology transfer*. One might surmise from the various authors' references to technology transfer in the table and from institutional and policy-oriented organizations' definitions in the table that technology transfer is a process that includes—paraphrasing from the quotations in the table—the development of knowledge (e.g., inventions or innovations), intellectual property (e.g., patents), entrepreneurial activity, research and development (R&D) activity, and scientific outcomes (e.g., scientific publications). A take-away from Table 2.7 is that only a few of the definitions of technology transfer are explicit that technology transfer is not a process that occurs automatically; technology transfer is a process that involves a "purposive, conscious effort" (Gilmore and Price, 1969, p. 2) and re-evaluation and/or implementation (Bar-Zakay, 1971). Also, from the definitions in the table, one might be surprised that only one of the definitions about the technology transfer process involves activities at universities and research institutions given the acknowledgment by many of the importance of the Bayh-Dole Act (Leyden and Link, 2015).[17]

Table 2.7   Definitions of technology transfer

Author(s)	Definition
Doctors (1969, p. 12)	"Federal agencies have tended to interpret their technology transfer mission in terms of documentation and formal information dissemination."
Gilmore and Price (1969, p. 2)	"[Technology transfer is] a purposive, conscious effort to move technical devices, materials, methods, and/or information from the point of discovery or development to new users."
Bar-Zakay (1971, p. 214)	"When scientific or technological information generated and/used in one context is reevaluated and/or implemented in a different context, process is called technology transfer."
Comptroller General of the United States (1979, p. 5)	"[Technology transfer is] the secondary application of technology developed for a particular mission or purpose to fill different needs in another environment."
National Academy of Engineering (1974, p. 4)	"The process of collection, documentation, and successful dissemination of scientific and technological information to a receiver through a number of mechanisms, both formal and informal, passive and active."
Federal Coordinating Council for Science, Engineering, and Technology (1977, p. v)	"In its broadest sense, technology transfer encompasses the collection, documentation, of scientific and technical information, including data on the performance and costs of using technology; the transformation of research and technology into processes, products, and services that can be applied to public or private needs; and the secondary application of research or technology developed for a particular mission that fills a need in another environment."

Author(s)	Definition
Jolly and Creighton (1977, p. 78)	"[Technology transfer is] the acceptance by a user of a practice common elsewhere, or may be a different application of a given technique designed originally for another use."
Teich (1979, p. 5)	"There is single, unambiguous meaning to the term 'technology transfer.' In practice, the notion encompasses a variety of activities all of which aim to transform R&D into products, processes or services that can serve needs in the public or private sectors."
Tuma (1987, p. 404)	"Technology transfer means acquisition and adaptation of a technique from one country or industry to another and its application in the production process. The transfer becomes complete when the technique has been domesticated and utilized as an integral part of the domestic production economy."
Seely (2003, p. 8)	"Technology transfer [is] the processes and consequences of moving technological ideas, skills, processes, hardware, and systems across a variety of boundaries—national, geographic, social and cultural, or organizational and institutional ..."
National Science Foundation*	"Technology transfer is the process by which technology or knowledge developed in one place or for one purpose is applied and used in another place for the same or different purpose."
Association for University Technology Managers – AUTM**	"[Technology transfer is] about evaluating, protecting and transferring intellectual property from the lab to the marketplace, corporate engagement, start-up and entrepreneurial support, and economic development."
Federal Laboratory Consortium for Technology Transfer***	"Technology transfer is the process by which existing knowledge, facilities, or capabilities developed under federal R&D funding are utilized to fulfill public and private needs."
World Intellectual Property Organization****	"Technology transfer (TT) is a collaborative process that allows scientific findings, knowledge and intellectual property to flow from creators, such as universities and research institutions, to public and private users. Its goal is to transform inventions and scientific outcomes into new products and services that benefit society. Technology transfer is closely related to knowledge transfer."

Note: * https://www.nsf.gov/statistics/seind14/index.cfm/chapter-4/c4s8.htm, accessed October 28, 2022; ** https://autm.net/about-tech-transfer, accessed October 28, 2022; *** https://federallabs.org/about/what-is-tech-transfer/video-overview, accessed October 28, 2022; **** https://www.wipo.int/technology-transfer/en/index.html, accessed October 28, 2022. An earlier version of this table appeared in Hayter et al. (2023).

To explore the meaning of technology transfer, be the transfer from or to the public sector, I consider here if or how academic research related to technology transfer activity has changed over time. A starting assumption for the collection of data to characterize the evolution of the meaning of technology transfer as a research field is that authors are themselves an, if not the, appropriate source to define the scope of their research through their use of descriptive keywords.

The *Journal of Technology Transfer* (*JTT*) is arguably the primary, if not the only scholarly journal devoted exclusively to the study of technology transfer;

thus, I view the *JTT* as an appropriate source from which to obtain relevant data.[18,19] Springer Nature, the publisher of the *JTT*, graciously provided all of the keywords used by authors of online published papers (hereafter, published papers or simply papers) over the calendar years (hereafter, years) 2005 through 2021—a paper accepted for publication in the *JTT* is first published online and later published in a printed version of the journal.[20,21]

A total of 2,303 unique keywords (hereafter, keywords) were identified as being used by authors over the years 2005 through 2021. This number is a result of a systematic consolidation process of the keywords provided by Springer Nature. Examples of such consolidations are: singular and plural words were consolidated (e.g., science park to science parks), all spellings were adjusted to U.S. spellings (e.g., labour to labor), and keywords and abbreviations (e.g., research and development to R&D).

Figure 2.5 shows, by year, the number of keywords per published papers. Visually, the trend is mildly positive. A linear regression of a year variable on keywords per published papers yielded a positive slope coefficient of 0.043 ($p = 0.0017$) with $R^2 = 0.493$. Perhaps, and this is personal speculation, the scope of academic inquiry about the research topic of technology transfer has been getting slightly more complex and thus more keywords are needed as explanators per paper.

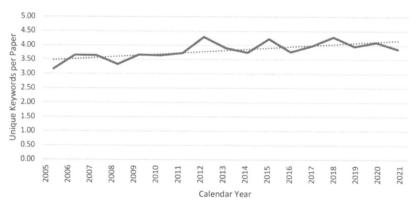

Note: The dotted line is an Excel-generated trend line.

Figure 2.5   *Unique keywords per published paper in the Journal of Technology Transfer, by calendar year 2005–21*

Table 2.8 shows the most frequently used keywords over the years 2005–21. The frequency of use of the keyword *technology transfer* should not be surprising, and neither should the use of the keyword *R&D*. Some readers may question what is meant by an author using the rather non-descriptive keyword *university*. While I cannot offer a precise explanation for the use of the keyword *university*, the frequency of use of that keyword might be interpreted to suggest that many academic research papers have been focused on university technology transfers to a greater extent than federal laboratory technology transfers (i.e., more focus on the Bayh-Dole Act than on the Stevenson-Wydler Act, both enacted in 1980).

For example, consider the uses of the keyword *university* in conjunction with other terms as shown in Table 2.9. The keywords *federal laboratory* or *federal lab* are not present in the data. Apparently, the public emphasis on technology transfer from federal laboratories, as emphasized by President Obama and President Trump, has not yet appeared in the academic literature published in the *JTT*.

Table 2.8   Most frequently used keywords in Journal of Technology Transfer papers, by calendar year 2005–21

Keyword	Number of Times Used by Authors
Technology transfer	171
University	61
R&D	46
University–industry collaboration	26
Absorptive capacity	23
Venture capital	19
University spinoffs	19
Small and medium-sized enterprises	18
Science parks	17
Start-ups	17
University technology transfer	17
Research collaboration	16
Business accelerator	15
Research	13
Knowledge	12
Technology commercialization	12
Gender	11
Germany	11
Productivity	11
Science	11
Performance	10
Technology	10
Technology transfer office	10
University–industry linkages	10

Table 2.9   *Use of variations of university as a keyword in Journal of Technology Transfer papers, by calendar year 2005–21*

Various Uses of the Keyword *University*	Number of Times Used by Authors
University	61
University–industry collaboration	26
University spinoffs	19
University technology transfer	17
University–industry linkages	10
University patenting	9
University patents	4
University research	4
University spinoffs	4
University technology commercialization	4
University–industry interaction	4
University–industry relations	4
University–industry partnerships	2
University–industry relationships	2
University commercialization	2
University mission	2
University research centers	2
University third mission	2

Note: In addition to the uses of the keyword *university* above, there are an additional 74 examples of a one-time use of a keyword that relates to a university (e.g., university technology initiatives, university-oriented seed funds).

As a final thought, the word *university* is not used in any of the definitions of technology transfer presented in Table 2.7, but the word *lab* is.

SUMMARY

The argument set forth by the European Commission in 2020 is that "knowledge transfers are an essential source of innovation" (European Commission, 2020, p. 6). This chapter expanded on that argument to show that traditional technology transfer mechanisms are a subset of knowledge transfer mechanisms, and they have a similar impact on innovation and economic growth as do knowledge transfers. Examples of both knowledge transfer and technology transfer mechanisms were discussed in a comparative light. Finally, as a segue to Chapter 3, I illustrated quantitatively how the concept of technology transfer has evolved over time using a keyword analysis based on information from the abstracts of published papers in the *JTT*.

In the following chapter, I offer a detailed history of the origin of the *concept* of technology transfer, and I place U.S. technology transfer activities and mechanisms in an historical context primarily beginning with the actions and activities of the American colonists. Also, I formally introduce the concept of public sector entrepreneurship as a framework for thinking about technology transfer legislation.

NOTES

1. An earlier version of the ideas expressed in this opening section are in Audretsch and Link (2019) and in Link and Van Hasselt (2023). Portions of the text in this section are paraphrased from these sources, and portions are included in this book under the presumption that the readers of these books will vary.
2. "If, in the history of epistemology, any sources of knowledge deserve to be called the classical basic sources, the best candidates are perception, memory, consciousness (sometimes called introspection), and reason (sometimes called intuition). Some writers have shortened the list under the heading, 'experience and reason'" (Audi, 2002, p. 72).
3. The following terms and ideas come directly from European Commission (2020).
4. As suggested in American Academy of Arts & Sciences (2020, p. 82): "There is no agreed-upon single measure of knowledge capital. However, several indicators are available that taken together provide an illuminating picture of relative status and overall trends. The most common metrics include publications (number, citations, and quality) and patents."
5. An excellent detailed history of NIST is in Cochrane (1966) and Schooley (2000). Briefly, the concept of the U.S. public sector's involvement in measurement standards traces to the Articles of Confederation signed on July 9, 1778, and the responsibility of "fixing the standard of weights and measures" is explicit in Article 1 of the Constitution of the United States. Jumping ahead by centuries, Lyman Gage, then Secretary of the Treasury under President William McKinley, championed the idea of a national standards laboratory. His efforts were instrumental in the passage of the March 3, 1901 Act (Public Law 177–56), often referred to as the Organic Act of 1901. The Organic Act of 1901 might reasonably be viewed as the first national effort in the United States to legislate the transfer of technology in the form of technical knowledge, or in some instances a technical artifact, from the public sector to all sectors in the economy. The Act renamed the existing Office of Standard Weights and Measures as the National Bureau of Standards (NBS). Jumping ahead again, but this time by decades, in the mid-1980s Congress considered "several initiatives to improve American competitiveness in world-wide markets" (Schooley, 2000, p. 613). These considerations were finally codified in the Omnibus Trade and Completeness Act of 1988 (Public Law 100–418). Stated therein: "The National Bureau of Standards since its establishment has served as the Federal focal point in developing basic measurement standards and related technologies, has taken a lead role in stimulating cooperative work among private industrial organizations in efforts to

surmount technological hurdles, and otherwise has been responsible for assisting in the improvement of industrial technology ... It is the purpose of this Act to rename the National Bureau of Standards as the National Institute of Standards and Technology [NIST] and to modernize and restructure that agency to augment its unique ability to enhance the competitiveness of American industry ..." A listing of the national metrology institutes in other countries is in Link (2022a).

6.   An earlier version of the material in this section is in Link (2023a).

7.   Swann's (2009) reference to market failure refers to the public good character- istics of measurement standards and the associated underinvestment in measure- ment standards research by the private sector.

8.   Another relevant event is the Covid-19 pandemic, but post-pandemic data are not available for consideration herein.

9.   For a discussion of the construction of a multifactor productivity index, see https://www.bls.gov/productivity/technical-notes/multifactor-productivity -method.pdf, accessed February 24, 2023.

10. See also Link (2023a).

11. This section draws directly from Hall et al. (2022).

12. See https://www.nist.gov/srm/about-nist-srms, accessed February 24, 2023.

13. As stated in the Act: "The National Bureau of Standards since its establishment has served as the Federal focal point in developing basic measurement standards and related technologies, has taken a lead role in stimulating cooperative work among private industrial organizations in efforts to surmount technological hurdles, and otherwise has been responsible for assisting in the improvement of industrial technology ... It is the purpose of this Act to rename the National Bureau of Standards as the National Institute of Standards and Technology [NIST] and to modernize and restructure that agency to augment its unique ability to enhance the competitiveness of American industry ..."

14. An excellent history of the activities related to the NBS's and NIST's role in the development and maintenance of Standards Reference Materials is by Rasberry (2003).

15. See https://www.nist.gov/mml/orm, accessed December 11, 2022. See also National Academies (2022) for an evaluation of the ORM and other offices and divisions in NIST's Material Measurement Laboratory.

16. When authors are from more than one federal agency, whole counting gives each agency full credit for the same publication When authors are from more than one federal agency, fractional counting assigns a portion or fraction of a publication to each agency. Thus, whole counts are not less than fractional counts. See Sivertsen et al. (2019) for a discussion of measurement methods for quantifying scientific contributions.

17. According to *The Economist* (2002, p. 3): "Possibly the most inspired piece of legislation to be enacted in America over the past half-century was the Bayh-Dole Act of 1980. Together with amendments in 1984 and augmentation in 1986, this unlocked all the inventions and discoveries that had been made in lab- oratories throughout the United States with the help of taxpayers' money. More than anything, this single policy measure helped to reverse America's precipitous slide into industrial irrelevance."

18. See the bibliographic analysis of journals in Noh and Lee (2019).

19. Keywords published with the abstract of a paper in the *JTT* are often phrases rather than individual words. I use the term *keyword* to refer to both author stated individual words as well as phrases.
20. Sincere thanks to Farhat Chowdhury for her assiduous effort to assemble the data provided by Springer Nature.
21. I define the year of publication to be the calendar year of the online publication of a paper. This method most closely identifies in time the year relevant to the author's choice of keywords. At the *JTT*, one's online published paper occurs within weeks of the paper's final acceptance.

3. Context, and an historical trace

INTRODUCTION

One might reasonably expect a chapter with a title such as this one to begin with the phrase, "The first use of the term *technology transfer* can be traced to ...," and one's expectations would be correct. However, after many months of reading and re-reading, I could not find evidence about how to complete such a sentence.[1] Working back in time, with the idea in mind that technology transfer refers to the movement of technical knowledge (see Table 2.7), I found several writings that might be viewed as a genesis point for a study of technology transfer. Those writings are summarized in the following sections.

HISTORICAL BEGINNINGS

To begin, Atrahasis, which means "extra wise," is described in Mesopotamian literature as the survivor, along with his wife, of the great flood that is recorded as occurring in the early third millennium, BC. Atrahasis was granted a form of immortality by the gods, presumably because of his diligence in preparing for the great flood (Dalley, 2008).

Regarding his preparations, as recorded on old Babylonian clay tablets dated to around 1700 BC, Atrahasis was told in a dream to dismantle his house and to build a boat, following the directed knowledge about technical means (Dalley, 2008, p. 30):

> Reject possessions, and save living things.
> The boat that you build ... Roof it like the Apsu[2]
> So that the Sun cannot see inside it!
> Make upper decks and lower decks.
> The tackle must be very strong,
> The bitumen[3] strong, to give strength.
> I shall make rain fall on you here, ...

The Old Testament offers a more complete story about the transfer of technology knowledge for building the ark. As written, God said to Noah (Lindsell, 1971, Genesis 11: 14–17):

> Make yourself an ark of gopher wood; make rooms in the ark, and cover it inside and out with pitch, this is how you are to make it: the length of the ark three hundred cubits, its breadth fifty cubit, and its height thirty cubits. Make a roof for the ark, and finish it to a cubit above; and set the door of the ark in its side; make it with lower, second, and third decks.

Some might date the first occurrence of the transfer of technology knowledge even earlier than the two flood stories above because there are more than a dozen such stories, legends, or myths about ancient floods in discovered writings from other civilizations.[4] A number of these accounts describe a higher being giving instructions (e.g., technical knowledge) to a person or persons on Earth about how to build a vessel to ensure survival during the floods.

Link and Oliver (2020) pointed out that there have been a number of contemporary scholars who have offered perspectives about the earliest examples of technology transfer.[5] To begin with, some have argued that technology transfer came about as a result of historical globalization. For example, Hyman and Renn (2012, p. 76) contend that as:

> … humans and their close hominid kin moved out of Africa … over half a million years [ago, and they took with themselves] knowledge related to stone tool technology that led to the creation of a wide range of Upper Paleolithic tool traditions.

The Hyman and Renn view has been reinforced by Potts (2012, p. 105). Potts offered the perspective that "knowledge and technology transfer [can clearly] be documented in the pre-literate past." These authors did not make reference to whether the knowledge transfer occurred in a pre- or post-flood period of time.

Seely (2003, p. 10) also noted that technology transfer is not a modern concept. He pointed to what is a more modern illustration of knowledge and technology transfer:[6]

> Many human activities involve technology transfer. Invention, trade, selling and buying, spying, and copying all involve transfers and diffusion, as do empire building and military conquest. Thus technology transfer is not a modern concept, as shown by historical episodes such as Venetian attempts to acquire the secret of Greek fire from the Byzantine navy during the late Middles Ages, the spread of the printing press across Europe after Gutenberg, or the British struggle to prevent the export of their steam engines and textile machinery; the core technologies of the industrial revolution …

EARLY U.S. KNOWLEDGE TRANSFERS AND TECHNOLOGY TRANSFERS

As I noted in Chapter 1, many will point to the Stevenson-Wydler Act of 1980 and the Bayh-Dole Act of 1980 as the foundational technology transfer legislation.[7] In this section of the chapter I discuss antecedent activity and legislation to these two Acts in an effort to present a more complete picture of U.S. actions that enveloped technology transfer as a process that impacts economic growth. A more formal historical trace begins with non-public sector actions from the colonial period of U.S. history (UNESCO, 1968, p. 9):[8]

> The organization and conduct of scientific and technological activities in the United States have undergone profound perhaps revolutionary changes [since World War II]. Yet, many characteristic features of today's scientific and technological enterprise were shaped by developments which occurred early in the nation's history.

One of the earliest records of knowledge transfer (in the areas of philosophy and natural history) might be dated to the first scientific society in the United States, the Boston Philosophical Society organized in 1683. In 1742, Benjamin Franklin founded the American Philosophical Society in Philadelphia, Pennsylvania. Its goal was to incorporate (UNESCO, 1968, p. 10):

> ... all of the then current branches of science [and to encourage] correspondence with residents of other colonies.

In 1769, it merged with another of Franklin's creations, the American Society for Promoting Useful Knowledge (UNESCO, 1968, p. 10):[9]

> ... which met in Philadelphia for the purpose of promoting useful knowledge ... [This merger gave the American Philosophical Society] new vigor and initiated a series of scientific activities that solidified its mission.

Thomas Jefferson served as president of the American Philosophical Society from 1797 to 1815. As President of the United States (1801–1809), he was committed to scientific endeavors and (UNECSO, 1968, p. 11):

> ... his conviction that the promotion of the general welfare depended heavily upon advances in scientific knowledge.

To wit, in 1803 Jefferson committed federal moneys to sponsor the Lewis and Clark expedition as previously noted (UNECSO, 1968, p. 11):

> This action set three precedents which were to prove significant in future scientific activities: the provision of federal funds for a scientific endeavor; the designation of

scientific exploration as a legitimate activity of the military; and the authorization of a governmental scientific expedition beyond the territorial boundaries of the United States.

In a broad sense, Jefferson's actions in this regard might be considered one of the founding actions of the United States to define that the Nation has a role in the discovery and sharing (i.e., transferring) of new knowledge.

Jefferson's commitment to the discovery and sharing of new knowledge was not a unique public sector action. For example, in 1846, Congress chartered the Smithsonian Institution from the $500,000 gift given by James Smithson to the United States (UNESCO, 1968, p. 12):

> ... to found in Washington, D.C. an institution for the purpose of *increasing and diffusing knowledge* [emphasis added] among men.

Other examples of the U.S. public sector's commitment to knowledge and technology transfers are seen through the establishment of the U.S. Department of Agriculture by President Abraham Lincoln on May 15, 1862. Three such noteworthy examples follow.

On July 2, 1862, Congress passed An Act Donating Public Lands to the Several States and Territories which May Provide Colleges for the Benefit of Agriculture and the Mechanic Arts, also known as the Morrill Act:[10]

> Be it enacted by the Senate and House of Representatives of the United States of America in Congress assembled, That there be granted to the several States, for the purposes hereinafter mentioned, an amount of public land, to be apportioned to each State a quantity equal to thirty thousand acres for each senator and representative in Congress ... And be it further enacted, That all moneys derived from the sale of the lands aforesaid by the States ... shall be invested in stocks of the United States, or of the States, or some other safe stocks, yielding not less than five per centum upon the par value of said stocks; and that the moneys so invested shall constitute a perpetual fund, the capital of which shall remain forever undiminished, (except so far as may be provided in section fifth of this act), and the interest of which shall be inviolably appropriated, by each State which may take and claim the benefit of this act, to the endowment, support, and maintenance of at least one college where the leading object shall be, without excluding other scientific and classical studies, and includ-ing military tactics, to teach such branches of learning as are related to agriculture and the mechanic arts ... in order to promote the liberal and practical education of the industrial classes in the several pursuits and professions in life.

On March 2, 1887, Congress passed An Act to Establish Agricultural Experiment Stations in Connection with the Colleges Established in the Several States, also known as the Hatch Act:[11]

> Be it enacted by the Senate and House of Representatives of the United States of America in Congress assembled, That in order to aid in acquiring and diffusing among the people of the United States useful and practical information on subjects connected with agriculture, and to promote scientific investigation and experiment respecting the principles and applications of agricultural science, there shall be established under [the Morrill Act] ... a department to be known and designated as an "agricultural experiment station." ... it shall be the object and duty of said experiment stations to conduct original researches or verify experiments on the physiology of plants and animals; the diseases to which they are severally subject, with the remedies for the same; the chemical composition of useful plants at their different stages of growth; the comparative advantages of rotative cropping as pursued under the varying series of crops; the capacity of new plants or trees for acclimation; the analysis of soils and water; the chemical composition of manures, natural or artificial, with experiments designed to test the comparative effects on crops of different kinds; the adaptation and value of grasses and forage plants; the composition and digestibility of the different kinds of food for domestic animals; the scientific and economic questions involved in the production of butter and cheese; and such other researches or experiments bearing directly on the agricultural industry of the United States as may in each case be deemed advisable ...

And, on May 8, 1914, Congress passed An Act to Provide for Cooperative Agricultural Extension Work between the Agricultural Colleges in the Several States, also known as the Smith-Lever Act:[12]

> Be it enacted by the Senate and House of Representatives of the United States of America in Congress assembled, That in order to aid in diffusing among the people of the United States useful and practical information on subjects relating to agriculture, uses of solar energy with respect to agriculture, home economics, and rural energy, and to encourage the application of the same, there may be continued or inaugurated in connection with the college of colleges in each State, Territory, or possession, now receiving, or which may hereafter receive, the benefits of [the Morrill Act] ... agricultural extension work which shall be carried on in cooperation with the United States Department of Agriculture ...

There are notable passages in these three foundational Acts that underscore the Nation's commitment to the public sector's support of knowledge and technology transfer. For example, in the Morrill Act, it is stated "to promote the liberal and practical education" of individuals; in the Hatch Act, it is stated "to conduct original researches or verify experiments ... bearing directly on the agricultural industry of the United States"; and in the Smith-Lever Act, it is stated "*diffusing* [emphasis added] among the people of the United States useful and practical information on subjects relating to agriculture." Implicit in these three Acts, and in the excerpted passages just above, is that the public sector is funding and providing such knowledge to society because it was believed that the private sector or the states would not be able to do the same. In other words, these three Acts are examples of the public sector responding to market failure (see Chapter 1).

Other notable legislation included the establishment of the National Academy of Sciences in 1863; the passage of the National Port Quarantine Act in 1878 for the public sector to support programs to study the origin of epidemic diseases and methods for preventing their spread; and the Pure Food and Drug Act was passed in 1906 to establish laboratory standards (public sector supported purity knowledge flowing to society).[13,14]

PUBLIC SECTOR ENTREPRENEURSHIP

The above-mentioned public sector (governmental agencies and Congress) initiatives fall under the rubric of being actions of public sector entrepreneurship.[15] Following Leyden and Link (2015, p. 14), public sector entrepreneurship can be defined as:

[P]ublic sector entrepreneurship refers to innovative public policy initiatives that generate greater economic prosperity by transforming a status quo economic environment into one that is more conducive to economic units engaging in creative activities in the face of uncertainty.

Or, as rephrased by Hayter et al. (2018, p. 682):

Public-sector entrepreneurship refers to the formation of innovative public-sector initiatives that transform a status quo social and economic environment into one that is more conducive to creative change in the face of uncertainty.

One of the more visible public sector entrepreneurs who spearheaded a transformation of the status quo with regard to the publicness of public sector knowledge was Vannevar Bush (who was briefly referenced in Chapter 1).[16] Vannevar Bush was born in 1890 in Everett, Massachusetts. Educationally, Bush graduated from Tufts College in 1913, and he received the Ph.D. from the Massachusetts Institute of Technology (MIT) in 1916. Skipping ahead in time—although one can read in Zachary's (1997) excellent biography of Bush and his experiences prior to being active in Washington, DC—I emphasize here Bush's Washington, DC experiences because they exemplify his commitment to the transfer and broad use of knowledge developed in one way or another by the public sector.

In 1938, while holding the offices of vice president of MIT and Dean of its School of Engineering, Bush was appointed to the National Advisory Committee for Aeronautics (NACA).

In 1939, Bush arrived in Washington, DC, where he became president of the Carnegie Institution of Washington on January 1. Bush arrived in Washington, DC with confidence about his ability to initiate change.

The National Academy of Science was the premier assemblage of scientists at the time, and its members had to be won over to the idea that government support of research, basic research in particular, was for the good of the Nation and that the military was not the only organizational structure to advance defense innovations (Zachary, 1997, pp. 106, 109):

> [Bush had] confidence that military men would accommodate scientists. But would scientists accept military rules? Only a new organization, free of the legacy of mistrust that had plagued past collaborations between researchers and the military, could satisfy the needs of the moment. Only Bush had a neck stiff enough to run it.

The next step was for Bush to meet with President Roosevelt and to champion himself and his ideas. A meeting was scheduled for Bush to meet with the President in early June 1939. This meeting would allow Bush to act, through this opportunity, on his perception that having government support research was for the common good. By the end of Bush's June 12 15-minute meeting with President Roosevelt, the President had agreed to the formation of the National Defense Research Committee, and for the Committee to (Zachary, 1997, p. 115):

> ... correlate and support scientific research on mechanisms and devices of warfare [and to support] with funds for office staff, and for financing research in laboratories of educational and scientific institutions or industry.

The rapidity with which the President agreed to the formation of the National Defense Research Committee was possibly due to the logical and pervasive way that Bush proposed it, as well as to the President's own concerns about the role, if any, that the United States would have in World War II.

The conclusion that I draw from Bush's meeting with President Roosevelt and the President's almost immediate positive response to Bush's ideas is that Bush perceived an opportunity to change the status quo through a new approach for government support of defense research that included the expertise of civilian researchers. In May 1941, President Roosevelt approved Bush's request for the formation of the Office of Scientific Research and Development (OSRD). The OSRD (Wiesner, 1979, p. 97):

> ... was a remarkable invention, but the most significant innovation was the plan by which, instead of building large government laboratories, contracts were made with universities and industrial laboratories for research appropriate to their capabilities ... Bush believed that World War II could be won only through advances in technology, and he proved to be correct.

This office became a funding vehicle for Bush's research agenda, implemented through contracted scientists, because it would receive funds directly from Congress. As explained by Zachary (1997, p. 133):

> Bush [as director of the OSRD] now had the authority to build small batches of weapons and equipment created by his researchers ... Bush could go ahead with production himself, demonstrate the weapon and then dare the service [i.e., the Army and the Navy] to ignore it.

Bush utilized institutional laboratories and the resources of government agencies through the OSRD's support of federal research centers. The first such federal research center was the Radiation Laboratory at MIT, which was operational before the OSRD was officially formed (Dale and Moy, 2000). These federal research centers were soon referred to as Federal Contract Research Centers (FCRCs) because their research programs were funded through federal contracts and because their employees—both their scientists and staff—were not federal employees (Link, 2022b). The next research center was the Naval Operations Research Group, which later became the Center for Naval Analysis (Carnegie Mellon University, 2017; Link, 2022b). These research centers represented the organizational harbinger of what eventually was to become (in 1967) Federally Funded Research and Development Centers (FFRDCs).

According to Link (2021, p. 577):

> FFRDCs became a research infrastructure to assist the government make cost effective choices in technology development, policy formation, systems acquisition and integration, and other vital elements of government operations (OTA, 1995). Many scientists after the war did not want to move to military laboratories or did not want to be government employees. They saw benefits being in a university setting or an industrial setting. Thus, FFRDCs were in practice a vehicle through which the federal government could capture this base of scientific knowledge. Fundamentally, FFRDCs facilitate cost effectiveness by emphasizing (Carnegie Mellon University, 2017: 27): "a commitment to the public interest, a long-term horizon, and an organizational structure outside of and apart from government, ensuring an absence of conflicts of interest."

A hallmark of Bush's tenure in the Roosevelt Administration was the organizational structure he assembled to harness the brainpower of civilian researchers. To that point (Zachary, 1997, p. 142):

> Bush's singular contribution to [a] "real and tough world" would not be to build more powerful bombs, but to organize the experts who would.

And stated differently and with keeping to the theme of this book, a hallmark of Bush's tenure in the Roosevelt Administration was to create an organizational structure conducive to incentivizing an inward flow of knowledge, that is, to incentivize the transfer of knowledge from contracted university and/or industrial scientists to those in federal laboratories. The FFRDCs would then become market failure delimiting vehicles for an outward flow of knowledge to society through publications, technologies, and post-doctoral students (post-docs) who have gained reflection and sensations.

Table 3.1 shows the number of post-docs at FFRDCs, by fiscal year. Knowledge and/or technology transfers are embodied in these individuals. The data are insufficient to offer a generalization about the social importance of FFRDC post-docs, but the fact that the number of post-docs has been increasing over the past decade suggests that there is likely an increasing demand for such opportunities and perhaps a realization within the federal laboratories that the use of budgeted resources toward this end is for the commonweal.

Table 3.1   *Post-docs at Federally Funded Research and Development Centers (FFRDCs), by fiscal year FY2010–FY2021*

Fiscal Year	Number of Post-docs
2010	3,011
2011	–
2012	2,793
2013	2,613
2014	–
2015	2,696
2016	–
2017	2,975
2018	–
2019	3,335
2020	–
2021	3,637

Source: https://ncses.nsf.gov/pubs/nsf22336?utm_medium=email&utm_source=govdelivery, accessed October 26, 2022.

Science—the Endless Frontier

Arguably, one of the most well-known publications of Bush was *Science—the Endless Frontier* (1945). Therein, Bush refers to the importance of federal knowledge and technology transfers, and I have noted such references by President Roosevelt and by Bush in italics below.

On November 17, 1944, President Roosevelt wrote to Bush (Bush, 1945, pp. 3–4):

DEAR DR. BUSH: The Office of Scientific Research and Development, of which you are the Director, represents a unique experiment of team-work and cooperation in coordinating scientific research and in applying existing scientific knowledge to the solution of the technical problems paramount in war. Its work has been conducted in the utmost secrecy and carried on without public recognition of any kind; but its tangible results can be found in the communiques coming in from the battle-fronts all over the world. Some day the full story of its achievements can be told.

There is, however, no reason why the lessons to be found in this experiment cannot be profitably employed in times of peace. *The information, the techniques, and the research experience developed by the OSRD and by the thousands of scientists in the universities and in private industry, should be used in the days of peace ahead for the improvement of the national health, the creation of new enterprises bringing new jobs, and the betterment of the national standard of living* [emphasis added].

It is with that objective in mind that I would like to have your recommendations on the following four major points:

First: What can be done, consistent with military security, and with the prior approval of the military authorities, to make known to the world as soon as possible the contributions which have been made during our war effort to scientific knowledge? *The diffusion of such knowledge should help us stimulate new enterprises, provide jobs for our returning servicemen and other workers, and make possible great strides for the improvement of the national well-being* [emphasis added].

Second: With particular reference to the war of science against disease, *what can be done now to organize a program for continuing in the future the work which has been done in medicine and related sciences* [emphasis added]? The fact that the annual deaths in this country from one or two diseases alone are far in excess of the total number of lives lost by us in battle during this war should make us conscious of the duty we owe future generations.

Third: What can the Government do now and in the future to aid research activities by public and private organizations? The proper roles of public and of private research, and their interrelation, should be carefully considered.

Fourth: Can an effective program be proposed for discovering and *developing scientific talent in American youth* [emphasis added] so that the continuing future of scientific research in this country may be assured on a level comparable to what has been done during the war?

New frontiers of the mind are before us, and if they are pioneered with the same vision, boldness, and drive with which we have waged this war we can create a fuller and more fruitful employment and a fuller and more fruitful life.

I hope that, after such consultation as you may deem advisable with your associates and others, you can let me have your considered judgment on these matters as soon as convenient—reporting on each when you are ready, rather than waiting for completion of your studies in all.

On July 5, 1945, Bush submitted his report to President Harry Truman.[17] In his letter of transmittal he wrote (Bush, 1945, p. 3):

> A single *mechanism* [emphasis added] for implementing the recommendations of the several committees is essential. In proposing such a mechanism, I have departed somewhat from the specific recommendations of the committees, but I have since been assured that the plan I am proposing is fully acceptable to the committee members.
>
> The pioneer spirit is still vigorous within this nation. Science offers a largely unexplored hinterland for the pioneer who has the tools for his task. The rewards of such exploration both for the Nation and the individual are great. Scientific progress is one essential key to our security as a nation, to our better health, to more jobs, to a higher standard of living, and to our cultural progress.

The "mechanism" to which Bush referred in his letter of transmittal was a National Research Foundation (Bush, 1945, p. 25):

> It is my judgment that the national interest in scientific research and scientific education can best be promoted by the creation of a National Research Foundation.
>
> The National Research Foundation should develop and promote a national policy for scientific research and scientific education, should support basic research in nonprofit organizations [i.e., universities], should develop scientific talent in American youth by means of scholarships and fellowships, and should by contract and otherwise support long-range research on military matters.
>
> Responsibility to the people, through the President and Congress, should be placed in the hands of, say nine Members, who should be persons not otherwise connected with the Government and not representative of any special interest, who should be known as National Research Foundation Members, selected by the President on the basis of their interest in and capacity to promote the purposes of the Foundation.

Bush's proposed National Research Foundation echoed the premise behind President Roosevelt's third question that was quoted above:

> What can the Government do now and in the future to aid research activities by public and private organizations? The proper roles of public and of private research, and their interrelation, should be carefully considered.

As suggested by Zachary (1997), this question might have presupposed an answer that Bush had previously given. Bush had previously (McDougall, 1985, pp. 79–80):

> ... impressed on the President the need to maintain autonomy for scientists lest their work be squelched or misguided by military supervisors ... The OSRD would con-

tract out most of its programs to universities, deemphasizing federal laboratories in favor of tapping the talents of society as a whole ... The obvious solution to ongoing federal R&D, and the one favored by Bush, was to extend something like the OSRD into peacetime ... [b]ut the difficulties of such a plan came to light in the proposed legislation of Senator Harley M. Kilgore ...[18]

A Congressional science policy study (Task Force on Science Policy, 1986, p. 26) wrote about this point of time in history, and thus the Task Force was indirectly writing about *Science—the Endless Frontier*:

A clear consensus was reached [by 1945] regarding the need for Government support for science and the desirability of establishing a science foundation. The areas of disagreement corresponded to the differences expressed earlier between Kilgore and Bush, namely the organization of the foundation, the distribution of funding [i.e., to basic and applied research (Kilgore) or only to basic research (Bush)], the role of social sciences [which Bush did not want to fund], and patent policy [about ownership of government funded research].

Bush later wrote, although not as a direct response to the Task Force on Science Policy, about his views on basic research versus applied research (1949, pp. 5–6):

What science produces, in the way of applications within its own changing limitations, depends upon what is desired by authority, by those who rule or represent the people. Pure science [i.e., basic research] may go its own way if it is allowed to do so, exploring the unknown with no thought other than to expand the boundaries of fundamental knowledge. *But applied science [i.e., applied research], the intricate process by which new knowledge becomes utilized by the forces of engineering and industry, pursues the path pointed out to it by authority. In a free country, in a democracy, this is the path that public opinion wishes to have pursued, whether it led to new cures for man's ills, or new sources of a raised standard of living, or new ways of waging war* [emphasis added]. In a dictatorship the path is the one that is dictated, whether the dictator be an individual or a self-perpetuating group.

And Bush revisited more than a decade later this same theme about basic research (i.e., scientific knowledge) being the foundation of science, but this time his view was expressed in a more philosophical manner (Bush, 1967, p. 191):

Science has a simple faith, which transcends utility. Nearly all men of science, all men of learning for that matter, and men of simple ways too, have it in some form and in some degree. It is the faith that it is the privilege of man to learn to understand, and that this is his mission.

With the passing of President Roosevelt in 1945, the end of World War II, and the influence of the OSRD ending at the end of 1947, a number of Bush's ideas for a National Research Foundation changed in favor of some of Kilgore's ideas,[19] although *Science—the Endless Frontier* is heralded even today as being the "blueprint for government supported science through a central agency."[20] And perhaps in the years to come, Bush's report might be heralded as a blueprint for a public sector organization to fund research-based knowledge to transfer throughout the Nation.

As pointed out in Chapter 1, many view the first legislation that was specific to the transfer of codified publicly funded research and knowledge came with the passage of the Stevenson-Wydler Act of 1980. To that point, Congress stated in the 1980 Act (and this passage is repeated below because of its implicit reference to market failure):

> ... the Federal laboratories and other performers of federally funded research and development frequently provide scientific and technological developments of potential use to State and local governments and private industry [and they] should be made accessible to ... improve the economic, environmental, and social well-being of the United States ...

Given the historical trace discussed above, a more accurate statement might be that the Stevenson-Wydler Act of 1980 perhaps marked contemporary emphasis on the transfer of publicly funded research and knowledge. That said, there is more in *Science—the Endless Frontier* that heralds in such a theme. Bush (1945) wrote in his report what could have been a direct response to the above Congressional statement:

> Progress ... depends upon a *flow of new scientific knowledge* [my emphasis]. New products, new industries, and more jobs require continuous additions to knowledge of the laws of nature, and the *application of that knowledge to practical purposes* [emphasis added]. (pp. 4–5)

> It has been basic United States policy that Government should foster the *opening of new frontiers* [emphasis added] ... [S]cientific progress is, and must be, of vital interest to Government. Without scientific progress the national health would deteriorate; without scientific progress we could not hope for improvement in our standard of living or for an increased number of jobs for our citizens; and without scientific progress we could not have maintained our liberties against tyranny. (p. 9)

A CONTEMPORARY POLICY IMPETUS

As part of a broad Domestic Policy Review in 1979, initiated in part in response to the productivity slowdown in the early 1970s, and then again in the late 1970s and early 1980s, President Jimmy Carter emphasized the importance of the transfer of technical knowledge. The President's message to Congress was in response to the productivity slowdown throughout the U.S. economy:[21]

> Often, the information that underlies a technological advance is not known to companies capable of commercially developing that advance. I am therefore taking several actions to ease and *encourage the flow of technical knowledge* [emphasis added] and information. These actions include establishing the Center for the Utilization of Federal Technology at the National Technical Information Service to improve the transfer of knowledge from Federal laboratories; and, through the State and Commerce Departments, increasing the availability of technical information developed in foreign countries.

Also, the Subcommittee on Science, Research and Technology of the Committee on Science and Technology of the U.S. House of Representatives held a series of hearings in the summer of 1979 on the role of federal laboratories in domestic technology transfer. The Honorable George E. Brown, Jr., chairman of the subcommittee, stated (Committee on Science and Technology, 1979, p. 1):

> In discussing our agenda for the 96th Congress, the members of the subcommittee put the general question of innovation and productivity very high on the priority list of activities for the subcommittee. And they have recognized that the Federal laboratories represent a major resource for innovation in the public sector particularly, and has decided to focus its attention on that role.

In the hearing, Gerald E. Miller of the Pacific Northwest Innovation Group offered a pragmatic statement (Miller, 1979, pp. 44–5):

> In the past 7 years I have been associated with the federal laboratory technology transfer effort. I have seen the requests for assistance mushroom and it is only going to increase at a greater rate. In the past month, and in the coming 6 months, I or other FLC representatives, will be appearing at the annual meetings of four of the largest public interest groups to advise their members of the existence of the FLC and of our interest in helping them. And frankly this concerns me because I wonder if the primary voluntary assistance program under which most of the federal laboratories are now assisting state and local governments can adequately perform under this increased workload. The chronic problems, which in the past have only increased the difficulty of transferring federal laboratory technology to state and local governments, now are becoming acute and will, in my opinion, severely hamper this transfer in the future unless remedies are taken in the near future. And what are the necessary remedies required to eliminate these problems [?] In my opinion [one remedy is the] [e]stablishment of *a national policy or mandate requiring all federal laboratories to have as a part of their mission the transfer of their technology to state and local government* [emphasis added].

An important point to note is that all of the knowledge transfer and technology transfer actions by public sector entrepreneurs mentioned above occurred *prior* to the Stevenson-Wydler Act of 1980.

STEVENSON-WYDLER TECHNOLOGY INNOVATION ACT OF 1980

In response to President Carter's Domestic Policy Review, and in response to Congress' awareness and concern about the productivity slowdown and options about the role of federal laboratory technology transfer, Congress passed the Stevenson-Wydler Technology Innovation Act of 1980 (Public Law 96–480) in October 1980. This 1980 Act states that Congress finds and declares that:

> Technology and industrial innovation are central to the economic, environmental, and social well-being of citizens of the United States. Technology and industrial innovation offer an improved standard of living, increased public and private sector productivity, creation of new industries and employment opportunities, improved public services and enhanced competitiveness of United States products in world markets. Many new discoveries and advances in science occur in universities and Federal laboratories, while the application of this new knowledge to commercial and useful public purposes depends largely upon actions by business and labor. Cooperation among academia, Federal laboratories, labor, and industry, in such forms as technology transfer, personnel exchange, joint research projects, and others, should be renewed, expanded, and strengthened … No comprehensive national policy exists to enhance technological innovation for commercial and public purposes. There is a need for such a policy, including a strong national policy supporting domestic technology transfer and utilization of the science and technology resources of the Federal Government. It is in the national interest to promote the adaptation of technological innovations to State and local government uses. Technological innovations can improve services, reduce their costs, and increase productivity in State and local governments. The Federal laboratories and other performers of federally funded research and development frequently provide scientific and technological developments of potential use to State and local governments and private industry. These developments should be made accessible to those governments and industry. There is a need to provide means of access and to give adequate personnel and funding support to these means.

Thus, as stated, the purpose of the 1980 Act is:

> … to improve the economic, environmental, and social well-being of the United States by … promoting technology development through the establishment of centers for industrial technology … [and to encourage] the exchange of scientific and technical personnel among academia, industry, and Federal laboratories.

And the 1980 Act makes clear that it is the responsibility of each federal laboratory to establish an office as well as mechanisms to transfer its technology to those organizations that will benefit:

> It is the continuing responsibility of the Federal Government to ensure the full use of the results of the Nation's Federal investment in research and development. To this end the Federal Government shall strive where appropriate to transfer federally owned or originated technology to State and local governments and to the private sector ... Each Federal laboratory shall establish an Office of Research and Technology Applications. Laboratories having existing organizational structures which perform the functions of this section may elect to combine the Office of Research and Technology Applications within the existing organization.

Regarding the functioning of these offices:

> It shall be the function of each Office of Research and Technology Applications to prepare an application assessment of each research and development project in which that laboratory is engaged which has potential for successful application in State or local government or in private industry [and] to provide and disseminate information on federally owned or originated products, processes, and services having potential application to State and local governments and to private industry.

Thus, the Stevenson-Wydler Technology Innovation Act of 1980 made explicitly clear the technology transfer responsibilities of federal laboratories.

To enhance the technology transfer mission of federal laboratories, Congress amended the Stevenson-Wydler Act of 1980 in October 1986 with the passage of the Federal Technology Transfer Act of 1986 (Public Law 99–502). The 1986 Act states:

> Each Federal agency may permit the director of any of its Government-operated Federal laboratories to enter into cooperative research and development agreements [CRADAs] on behalf of such agency with other Federal agencies; units of State or local government; industrial organizations (including corporations, schools and partnerships, and limited partnerships, and industrial development organizations); public and private foundations; nonprofit organizations (including universities); or other persons (including licensees of inventions owned by the Federal agency); and to negotiate licensing agreements ... for Government-owned inventions made at the laboratory and other inventions of Federal employees that may be voluntarily assigned to the Government.

The 1986 Act also established the Federal Laboratory Consortium for Technology Transfer (FLC) (discussed in Chapter 4), with the National Bureau of Standards (NBS, which later became the National Institute of Standards and

Technology, NIST) acting as the host agency. As stated in the Act, the FLC would:

> ... develop and (with the consent of the Federal laboratory concerned) administer techniques, training courses, and materials concerning technology transfer to increase the awareness of Federal laboratory employees regarding the commercial potential of laboratory technology and innovations; furnish advice and assistance requested by Federal agencies and laboratories for use in their technology transfer programs (including the planning of seminars for small business and other industry); [and] provide a clearinghouse for requests, received at the laboratory level, for technical assistance from States and units of local governments, businesses, industrial development organizations, not-for-profit organizations including universities, Federal agencies and laboratories, and other persons.

To support the ability of federal laboratories to transfer their technologies to State and local governments and private industry (although on my reading of history the primary emphasis was to State and local governments), the Federal Technology Transfer Act of 1986 also facilitated technology transfer by permitting the laboratories to enter into CRADAs with public and private organizations. The Act made clear that government-owned, government-operated laboratories (GOGOs) could enter into CRADAs, but the Act was not specific about government-owned, contractor-operated laboratories (GOCOs). As defined by the Federal Laboratory Consortium for Technology Transfer (FLC, 2018, p. 5):[22]

> Federal labs are typically managed under two general models: the government-owned, government-operated (GOGO) model and the government-owned, contractor-operated (GOCO) model. GOGO laboratories are usually owned or leased by the federal government and staffed by federal employees who are supported by nonfederal contract employees. GOCO laboratories are institutions where the facilities and equipment are owned by the federal government, but the staff is employed by a private or public contractor that operates the laboratory under a contract with the federal government.

As an additional incentive for federal laboratory scientists to be proactive in the identification and transfer of their developed technologies, the 1986 Act stipulated that:

> ... any royalties or other income received by a Federal agency from the licensing or assignment of inventions under agreements entered into ... shall be retained by the agency whose laboratory produced the invention and shall be disposed of as follows: The head of the agency or his designee shall pay at least 15 percent of the royalties or other income the agency receives on account of any invention to the inventor (or co-inventors) if the inventor (or each such co-inventor) was an employee of the agency at the time the invention was made.

SUMMARY

In this chapter I have attempted to make the case that the Stevenson-Wydler Act of 1980 was not the first public policy to emphasize technology transfer from federal laboratories. In fact, history bears witness to many writings in prior decades (and centuries) that relate to the *concept* of technology transfer. Still, based on an analysis of information from published papers in the *Journal of Technology Transfer*, the concept of technology transfer is fluid.

Chapter 4 provides the context for how federal laboratories operationalized their role in technology transfer legislation beginning with the Stevenson-Wydler Act of 1980. This chapter also places the FLC in the position of being a unique organization or infrastructure that supports technology-based economic growth.

NOTES

1. What was interesting to me was that I found a number of journal articles that made reference to the concept of technology transfer in the title or in a major section heading, but never defined what technology transfer meant.
2. The word *Apsu* in Mesopotamian mythology refers to "the watery deep beneath the earth." See http://www.ancient-mythology.com/mesopotamian/apsu.php, accessed December 11, 2022.
3. "Bitumen ... is a black, oily, viscous form of petroleum, a naturally-occurring organic byproduct of decomposed plants." See https://www.thoughtco.com/bitumen-history-of-black-goo-170085, accessed December 11, 2022.
4. See https://www.mythoreligio.com/15-flood-myths-similar-to-the-story-of-noah-2/, accessed December 11, 2022.
5. Much of this section draws from Link and Oliver (2020).
6. Seely (2003) appropriately credited his sources to be Eisenstein (1980), Harris (1992), and Roland (1992). Seely (2003, p. 8) also makes the case that published research and "scholarly interest [in technology transfer] exploded after 1980." In October 1980, U.S. President Jimmy Carter signed Public Law 96–480, formally known as the Stevenson-Wydler Technology Innovation Act of 1980. This Act states: "It is the continuing responsibility of the Federal Government to ensure the full use of the results of the Nation's Federal investment in research and development. To this end the Federal Government shall strive where appropriate to transfer federally owned or originated technology to State and local governments and to the private sector." The ability of federal laboratories to transfer their technologies was enhanced by several amendments to the 1980 Act. The amendments are the Federal Technology Transfer Act of 1986, the National Technology Transfer and Advancement Act of 1995, and the Technology Transfer Commercialization Act of 2000. In December 1980, U.S. President Jimmy Carter signed Public Law 96–517, formally known as the University and Small Business Patent Protection Act of 1980 but informally known as the Bayh-Dole Act. This Act does not talk about technology transfer in the same context as the Stevenson-Wydler Act did. See Leyden and Link (2015) and Link

and Van Hasselt (2019) for a broader interpretation of the economic importance of the Bayh-Dole Act. See also Martin (2009) about the Bayh-Dole Act.

7.   For example, the title of the paper by Noh and Lee (2019) is "Where technology transfer research originated and where it is going: a quantitative analysis of literature published between 1980 and 2015." But, as discussed in Chapter 2, and elsewhere in this book, scholars were writing about technology transfer decades prior to 1980. Also, Rudolph (1994, pp. 133–4) points out, albeit with respect to patents as a technology transfer mechanism: "Long before Senator Stevenson (IL, D) and Congressman Sydler (NY, R) introduced the first version of their bill [in 1979] in the 95th Congress, many agencies, including the Department of Defense, the National Institutes of Health (NIH) and the National Science Foundation (NSF), already allowed contractors to retain patent rights to their inventions. Other agencies, such as the Department of Agriculture, the National Aeronautics and Space [Administration]."

8.   Historical examples of technology transfer in other cultures are in Inkster (2007).

9.   See https://philadelphiaencyclopedia.org/essays/american-philosophical-society/, accessed October 26, 2022.

10.   The Honorable Justin Smith Morrill (R) from Vermont served in the U.S. House of Representatives from 1855 to 1867, and he served in the U.S. Senate from 1867 to 1898.

11.   The Honorable William H. Hatch (D) from Missouri served in the U.S. House of Representatives from 1879 to 1895.

12.   The Honorable Michael Hoke Smith (D) from Georgia served in the U.S. Senate from 1911 to 1920. The Honorable Asbury Francis Lever (D) from South Carolina served in the U.S. House of Representatives from 1901 to 1919.

13.   These are only a few of the other examples highlighted in UNESCO (1968).

14.   See also Rosenberg's (1970) discussion of the transmission of technology in the 19th century.

15.   Much of this section draws from Link (2022b); the copyright to that publication resides with the author.

16.   This section draws directly from Link (2022b).

17.   President Roosevelt passed on April 12, 1945.

18.   For Kilgore's legislative opposition to Bush's view, see Bush (1949). See also Kevles (1977).

19.   Many, but not all, of Bush's conceptual ideas were modified by Steelman, the White House aid to President Truman, in *Science and Public Policy: A Program for the Nation*: https:// www .nsf.gov/ about/ history/ nsf50/ science _policy .jsp, accessed October 28, 2022).

20.   See https://www.nsf.gov/about/history/nsf50/nsf8816.jsp, accessed October 28, 2022.

21.   See President Carter's Industrial Innovation Initiatives Message to the Congress on Administration Actions and Proposals (October 31, 1979): http:// www .presidency.ucsb.edu/ws/index.php?pid=31628, accessed November 3, 2022.

22.   For more detailed information on GOGO and GOCO laboratories, see Bozeman and Wilson (2004) and Snyder and Thomas (undated).

4. The Federal Laboratory Consortium

BACKGROUND ON THE ECONOMY

The U.S. economy exhibited a number of downturns in the years following World War II. Table 4.1 dates five such periods, although the last two periods in the table are directly relevant to the topic of this chapter. When one couples these latter downturns with the productivity slowdown in the early and then again in the late 1970s and early 1980s, as illustrated in Figures 4.1 and 4.2 by the hashed bars,[1] one might presume that reviving economic growth was centerstage at that time and that economic growth became an agenda item for many federal agencies and Congressional committees. While it is well documented that the Stevenson-Wydler Act of 1980 was one such Congressional response to the productivity slowdown, there is also evidence of a parallel emphasis on technology transfer from federal laboratories to other agencies to ameliorate the consequences of the slowdown. More specifically, calls for intergovernmental sharing of federal laboratory technology as a means to deal with the economic slowdowns, and to reverse the downturns went beyond the messages of Bush (see Chapter 3).

Table 4.1   *Economy recessions after World War II*

Peak Year	Trough Year	Months from Perk to Trough
1953	1954	10
1957	1958	8
1960	1961	10
1969	1970	11
1973	1973	16

Source: National Bureau of Economic Research (NBER). See https://www.nber.org/research/data/us-business-cycle-expansions-and-contractions, accessed November 4, 2022.

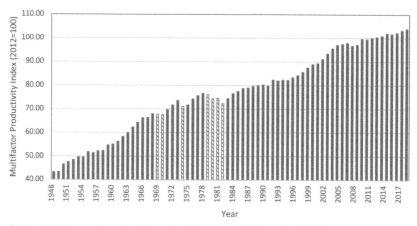

Source: https://www.bls.gov/mfp/mprdload.htm, accessed November 6, 2022.

Figure 4.1   *Multifactor productivity and periods of productivity*
                    slowdown in the economy

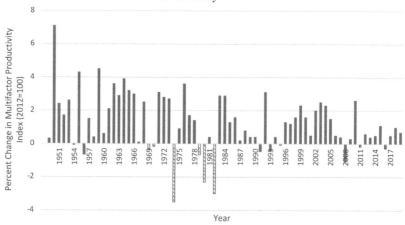

Source: https://www.bls.gov/mfp/mprdload.htm, accessed November 6, 2022.

Figure 4.2   *Changes in multifactor productivity and periods of*
                    productivity slowdown in the economy

On August 2, 1973, the Task Force on Intergovernmental Use of Federal R&D
Laboratories of the Committee on Federal Laboratories was established. Its
charge was to identify ways through which federal laboratories could improve
their technical assistance and support of government organizations (Federal

Council for Science and Technology, 1974). However, Richard W. Roberts, then Chairman of the Committee on Federal Laboratories, pointed out in the Introduction to the Federal Council for Science and Technology report *Intergovernmental Use of Federal R&D Laboratories* (Federal Council for Science and Technology, 1974, p. vii) the following:[2]

> To recognize the need for more effective intergovernmental utilization of Federal laboratories is one thing; to achieve it is another.

Perhaps Chairman Robert's comment is reflective of the findings in the 1973 Council of State Governments report, prepared under the sponsorship of the National Science Foundation. The study was undertaken (Council of State Governments, 1973, p. i):

> ... to examine the existing policies and practices applied to the external use of Federal R&D laboratories, and to review their potentials for assisting state and local governments.

The Council of State Governments report is referenced in the Federal Council for Science and Technology, published in 1974. The Council's report is detailed about the following barriers that exist for technology transfer from federal laboratories (Council of State Governments, 1973, p. 4):

> Despite good intentions and a favorable general policy climate, severe constraints limit the abilities of the Federal laboratories to strengthen technology applications in state governments.

For example (Council of State Governments, 1973, p. 13):

> A problem that arises in coupling Federal laboratory technology to the needs of civil agencies and governments is that of incompatibility. High technology may be too sophisticated for civil applications, without modifications and adaptations.

Relatedly, the Federal Council for Science and Technology (1974, p. 1) report noted:

> For some time the Nation has been experiencing rapid and accelerating changes in its public needs and priorities and an increase in accompanying technological problems ... The solution to these problems and needs must be sought across departmental, agency and private sector lines, thus making it necessary to achieve maximum flexibility in the use of existing [federal] laboratory capabilities ... In this context it should be axiomatic that every department and agency requiring scienfic and engineering study and the development of technical applications be required to fully consider the use of capabilities in existing Federal laboratories and federally-funded research and development centers prior to expending funds for the creation of new

or additional facilities. These laboratories represent not only a large and cumulative national investment in science facilities and equipment, but also a wide variety of specialized, in-place, scientific and engineering competencies and experiences.

Similarly, Linsteadt (1976, p. 107) wrote, with public-servant eyes on previous economic events and with expertise about the knowledge base that endowed federal laboratories:[3]

> It does not seem at all necessary to describe in any great detail the problems existing in our nation today. Energy, unemployment, high prices, and many other national concerns, which are equally as meaningful in keeping this nation strong, face all levels of government ... [F]ederal agencies [do] constitute a source for solutions to problems through the many federal laboratories. These laboratories contain a reservoir of technology plus the facilities, equipment, and capable professional people with which to address the many problems.

However, funding was also (and still is) a constraint. Technology transfer activities in federal laboratories were not a costless process, although it was a non-budgeted process. Relatedly, at that time, the Mansfield Amendment to the Military Authorization Act of 1969 also created a technology transfer-related problem (Task Force on Science Policy, 1986, p. 62):

> None of the funds authorized to be appropriated by this Act may be used to carry out any research project or study unless such a project or study has a direct or apparent relationship to a specific military function of operations.

It should be emphasized that in these early years, the focus of technology transfer from federal laboratories was on enhancing the mission and goals of *other* government agencies as well as the States themselves; the focus was not on enhancing the technological growth of private sector firms or organizations. For example, Linsteadt (1978, p. 2–2) pointed out the fact that in the early 1970s there was:

> ... one dominant theme for making the technical resources represented by the federal laboratories available to state and local governments. A greater return can be had on the taxpayer's investment in science and technology through more effective primary *and secondary* use of R&D results. State and local governments are very much aware that many of their problems can be solved only through the use of science and technology. However, these agencies cannot afford to invest large sums in R&D ...

To complement Linsteadt's comment above, the Comptroller General of the United States emphasized efficiencies associated with the sharing of technical knowledge (Comptroller General of the United States, 1979, p. 2):

> While there are many types of cooperation in research and development, interagency laboratory use is one effective means of avoiding duplicative efforts and efficiently using costly Federal facilities and skilled technical personnel. However, there is no Government-wide policy or coordinating mechanism which specifically addresses contracting by one Federal agency with the laboratories of another.

THE FEDERAL LABORATORY CONSORTIUM

The Federal Laboratory Consortium (FLC), while formalized through the Federal Technology Transfer Act of 1986 as discussed in Chapter 3, can be traced at least to the formation of the Department of Defense Technology Transfer Consortium. Linsteadt (1978, p. 2–2) documents that the beginning of the FLC traces to 1971 when 11 Department of Defense laboratories met at the Naval Weapons Center to discuss methodologies for how military technological knowledge could be used elsewhere in the economy:[4]

> The Consortium [i.e., the FLC] actually had its beginning in the summer of 1971. At that time eleven Department of Defense laboratories met at the Naval Weapons Center, China Lake, California, to determine common methodologies in finding greater use for the technical knowledge developed for military purposes. These eleven labs formed an informal affiliation called the DoD Technology Transfer Laboratory Consortium.

One might be struck by the phrase in the Linsteadt statement just above, "finding greater use for the technical knowledge developed for military purposes." Recall, from Chapter 3, President Roosevelt's charge to Bush in 1944:

> There is, however, no reason why the lessons to be found [through the work of the Office of Scientific Research and Development, the OSRD] cannot be profitably employed in times of peace. The information, the techniques, and the *research experience developed by the OSRD* [emphasis added] and by the thousands of scientists in the universities and in private industry, should be used in the days of peace ahead for the improvement of the national health, the creation of new enterprises bringing new jobs, and the betterment of the national standard of living.

Linsteadt (1976, p. 110) quoted in his overview of the Department of Defense Technology Transfer Consortium, the Consortium's operation policy:

> The Department of Defense laboratories are a source of technology for the solution of those civil sector problems which are amenable to technological solutions. The primary role of the in-house laboratories is to provide a research and development

base for the development of systems required to fulfill the national security mission of the Department of Defense. However, these laboratories can serve a vital secondary role in the adaptation of technology to other fields and areas of need to the extent that it does not adversely impact on the primary Department of Defense mission. A consortium of Department of Defense laboratories is formed for the purpose of coordinating interactions with other federal agencies and technology users at the federal, state, and local level, and of coordinating the efforts in this endeavor. The Technology Transfer Consortium is an association of Department of Defense laboratories working together through an informal affiliation. The main thrust of the consortium activity is through the individual and cooperative efforts of the laboratories involved, with an emphasis on the transfer and adaptation of technology through person-to-person mechanism.

However, the DOD was not the first agency to emphasize the transfer of publicly funded technical knowledge and technology; NASA was. According to Metcalf (1994, p. 14):

The National Aeronautics and Space Administration (NASA) launched a program back in 1958 to promote the transfer and application of its technology and expertise outside its own arena. The basis of its program was the 1958 National Aeronautics and Space Act. The language of that act required that the widest possible utilization be promoted in a variety of fields.

The National Aeronautics and Space Act of 1958 (Public Law 85–568) documents Metcalf's statement above. As stated in the Act of 1958:

Be it enacted by the Senate and House of Representatives of the United States of America in Congress assembled, That ... The aeronautical and space activities of the United States shall be conducted so as to contribute materially to one or more of the following objectives: ... (4) The establishment of long-range studies of the potential benefits to be gained from, the opportunities for, and the problems involved in the *utilization* [emphasis added] of aeronautical and space activities for peaceful and scientific purposes ... [And] (8) The most effective *utilization* [emphasis added] of the scientific and engineering resources of the United States, with close cooperation among all interested agencies of the United States in order to avoid unnecessary duplication of effort, facilities, and equipment.

Comstock and Lockney (2007, pp. 1–2) also wrote about NASA's commitment to technology transfer as NASA approached its 50th anniversary:

... we reflect on a proud history of achievements that have pushed back boundaries and opened new frontiers for all humanity in the exploration of our solar system and our understanding of the universe and our place in it. New technologies have arisen during this journey, developed of necessity, and spurred by the innovative spirit that answers the call of doing the impossible. In the wake of a half-century of advancement, myriad technologies—without which the limits of aeronautics and space could not have been challenged—have found other uses. From the mundane to the sublime, these technologies have become part of the fabric of our everyday life, driving innovation, helping the economy, and adding to the quality of life not only in the United States, but around the world ... *Technology transfer* [emphasis added] has been a mandate for NASA since it was established in 1958 by the National Aeronautics and Space Act. National leaders at that time recognized that NASA would play an important role in driving technology development to achieve its goals in space and aeronautics, and that those technologies could provide important benefits for the Nation.

The word *utilization* in the above statement quoted from the National Aeronautics and Space Act is what Metcalf referred to as the promotion of the "transfer and application" of NASA technology. Metcalf went on to state (1994, p. 14):

NASA's mandate did not result in similar activity in the laboratories of the other government agencies, nor did it provide for any policy or legislation for them.

The theme of transferring technical knowledge from federal laboratories was also a part of the thinking of then President Richard Nixon.[5] In a special message to Congress on science and technology on March 16, 1972, as part of his American Presidency Project, President Nixon stated:

The ability of the American people to harness the discovering of science in the service of man has always been an important element of our national progress ... I am therefore calling today for a strong new effort to marshal science and technology in the work of strengthening our economy and improving the quality of our life. And I am outlining ways in which the Federal Government can work as a more effective partner in this great task. The importance of technological innovation has become dramatically evident in the past few years [see the periods of productivity slowdown in Table 4.1 and Figures 4.1 and 4.2]. For one thing, we have come to recognize that such innovation is essential to improving our economic productivity ... As we face the new challenges of the 1970s, we can draw upon a great reservoir of scientific and technological information and skill—the result of the enormous investments which both the Federal government and private enterprise made in research and development in recent years ... We must appreciate that the progress we seek requires a new partnership in science and technology—one which brings together the Federal Government, private enterprise, State and local governments, and our universities and research centers in a coordinated, cooperative effort to serve the national interest.

And to the mission of the early-on DOD laboratories, which was focused on intergovernmental transfers, and to the mission of the FLC, which was and still is more broadly focused, President Nixon went on to say:

The role of the Federal Government in shaping American Science is pivotal. Of all our Nation's expenditures on research and development, 55 percent are presently funded by the Federal Government ... I believe the Government has a responsibility *to transfer the results of its research and development activities to wider use in the private sector* [emphasis added].

The FLC's current website refers indirectly to its mission:[6]

> The FLC was formed in 1974, in response to the economic challenges of the 1970s, to help boost U.S. productivity by promoting the movement of technologies out of federal labs and into the private sector—a process called technology transfer. Policymakers embraced the idea that commercializing federal technologies would create new jobs and new domestic markets, and the Stevenson-Wydler Technology Innovation Act of 1980 and the Federal Technology Transfer Act of 1986 helped make this possible. The FLC was formally chartered by the Federal Technology Transfer Act to promote technology transfer through collaborative partnerships with nonfederal organizations such as private business, academia, and state and local governments.

In the early years, the FLC was focused on the needed intergovernmental use of federally funded technical knowledge. According to Linsteadt (1978, p. 2–2):

> The basic objective of the FLC [was initially] to design, develop and implement, on a systematic basis, mechanisms which facilitate the application of unique mission agency federal laboratory capabilities to nationally defined problems so that publicly funded R&D resources are made widely available on a cost-effective and timely basis. Special *emphasis is given to problems associated with the intergovernmental use of federal laboratories and centers for the solution of domestic problems at state and local government levels* [emphasis added] and integration with the program elements and R&D planning process of federal agencies.

And the current mission statement of the FLC still remains focused on intergovernmental knowledge transfers, but it also includes a focus on technology transfer for the benefit of the U.S. economy as a whole:[7,8,9]

> Every federal agency has a mission, and each lab's technology transfer efforts are intended to help achieve that mission. By helping to facilitate federal technology transfer, the FLC is also supporting each agency's mission. In addition, the FLC has its own mission: *To increase the impact of federal laboratories' technology transfer for the benefit of the U.S. economy, society, and national security* [emphasis added].

But, to the importance of technology transfer benefitting the entire economy, which includes the private sector, the FLC states that it executes its mission by increasing the impact of federal technology transfer broadly by:[10,11]

- Promoting federal R&D and the significant economic benefits of tech transfer among government, *industry, academia, and other external partners* [emphasis added]. The FLC promotes federal T2 [technology transfer] activities and suc-

cesses through the FLC awards program, Labs in Action, the FLC Planner, and Lab Tech in Your Life.
- Educating federal tech transfer professionals and their partners about commercialization strategies through training opportunities and reference materials. The FLC offers in-person and online training for anyone—from novice to expert—to expand their T2 knowledge for improved understanding and easy navigation of the federal commercialization process.
- Facilitating federal laboratories' tech transfer goals via FLC-created tools and services that enable a partnership-driven path for getting technologies from lab to market. The FLC makes prospective partners aware of federal technologies available for licensing and facilitates connections between federal labs and nonfederal partners.

The FLC currently uses several metrics to measure the effectiveness of fulfilling its mission. Outcomes used to measure the impact of federal technology transfer include:[12]

- Number of inventions disclosed and patents issued. These indicate a lab's commitment to protecting its intellectual property, which can be attractive to a prospective partner.
- Number of licenses giving a partner access to a lab's technology. The specific terms of a license provide incentives for the partner to invest the resources needed to develop and commercialize the technology.
- Income from licenses. This can include royalties, license issue fees, minimum annual royalties, paid-up license fees, and reimbursement for goods and services provided by the lab to the licensee, including patent costs. Income from licenses is typically reinvested in a lab's research and development efforts, which in turn promotes future technology transfer opportunities.
- Number of agreements with nonfederal partners. These can include research collaboration agreements (RCAs), cooperative research and development agreements (CRADAs), user facility agreements, material transfer agreements (MTAs), educational partnership agreements (EPAs), and partnership intermediary agreements (PIAs).

SUMMARY

This chapter provided context for how federal laboratories operationalized technology transfer legislation beginning with the Stevenson-Wydler Act of 1980. This chapter also places, through an overview of institutional history, the FLC in the position of being a unique organization or infrastructure that supports the technology-based economic growth of the Nation.

Chapter 5 presents a descriptive and statistical analysis of federal laboratory technology transfer mechanisms and metrics for each of the 11 major federal agencies. The statistical analysis is motivated by an allocation model that associates federal basic research and applied research allocations (i.e., financial inputs) with various knowledge transfer and technology transfer mechanisms (i.e., technical outputs).

NOTES

1. Many refer to the productivity slowdown as the periods of decline in multifactor productivity growth in the industrial sectors of the economy. Multifactor productivity (MFP) is widely regarded as a metric associated with a nation's technological growth. See Bozeman and Link (2014).
2. Nearly 50 years later, the National Academies of Sciences, Engineering, and Medicine (2022) is reflecting, albeit indirectly, on the profoundness of this statement.
3. Mr. George F. Linsteadt was a pioneer and champion of the Department of Defense Technology Transfer (DOD T2) program. Through the George F. Linsteadt Award for Excellence in Technology Transfer, "the Office of the Under Secretary of Defense for Research and Engineering (OUSDR&E) recognizes professionals who embody the vision and spirit of Mr. Linsteadt and his proactive legacy in the shaping of the DOD's T2 community, and highlights initiatives that have had a significant impact on the DoD T2 program." See https://rt.cto.mil/george-f-linsteadt-award-for-excellence-in-technology-transfer/, accessed November 25, 2022. When writing these statements, Linsteadt was Chairman of the Federal Laboratory Consortium.
4. Metcalf (1994) substantiates this DOD knowledge transfer effort. See also Linsteadt (1976, p. 109).
5. See https://www.presidency.ucsb.edu/documents/special-message-the-congress-science-and-technology, accessed November 25, 2022.
6. See https://federallabs.org/about/who-we-are/history, accessed November 5, 2022.
7. See https://federallabs.org/about/who-we-are/mission-vision, accessed November 5, 2022.
8. For an overview of the structure of the FLC, see FLC (2020).
9. Surprisingly, at least to me, is the omission of a discussion of the FLC in the National Science and Technology Council's (2021) report on R&D infrastructure.
10. See https://federallabs.org/about/who-we-are/mission-vision, accessed November 5, 2022.
11. Examples of technology transfer to the private sector through a federal laboratory are discussed in GAO (2014).
12. See https://federallabs.org/about/who-we-are/mission-vision, accessed November 5, 2022.

5. Federal laboratory technology transfer mechanisms and metrics

INTRODUCTION AND BACKGROUND

This chapter focuses on trends in the so-called mirepoix of technology transfer channels or mechanisms: patents, licenses, and collaborative research efforts. The event that I focus on as a possible culprit to alter these trends is the Great Recession (December 2007–June 2009). In the years to come, as more data are collected by the Technology Partnerships Office at the National Institute of Standards and Technology (NIST), researchers might also focus on the Covid-19 pandemic as the culprit of emphasis.

Academic researchers and policy makers have traditionally emphasized patenting activity in federal laboratories. Perhaps the reason for this singular focus is the accessibility of patent data from the United States Patent and Trademark Office (USPTO). However, an emphasis on other technology transfer mechanisms recently gained/regained policy importance in response to President Obama's October 2011 Presidential Memorandum—Accelerating Technology Transfer and Commercialization of Federal Research in Support of High-Growth Businesses—as discussed in Chapter 1.

In November 2012, the Interagency Work Group on Technology Transfer (IAWGTT) issued a response to the President's October 2011 Memorandum.[1] Its response specifically mentioned the need for a more detailed reporting of Cooperative Research and Development Agreement (CRADA) activity, by agency, especially with regard to such partnerships with small businesses:

> … new metrics will be included to demonstrate and encourage collaboration with small businesses.

SELECTED TECHNOLOGY TRANSFER METRICS

Table 5.1 shows the number of patent applications filed with the U.S. Patent and Trademark Office (USPTO) over the fiscal years FY2003 through FY2019.[2] As defined in the Department of Commerce's (USDOC) *Guidance for Preparing Annual Agency Technology Transfer Reports* (2020, p. 10), a patent and a patent application are:[3]

> ... a legal document which provides protection to the ideas of any individual. Usually issued by the Patent Office of a country, the patent is granted to any firm or individual. This includes patents in which the Government-owned, Government-operated or Government-owned, Contractor-operated lab has ownership interest where the patent is jointly owned with another party regardless of which party leads the filing or licensing.
>
> A U.S. patent application [refers to a] non-provisional U.S. patent application filed at the United States Patent and Trademark Office. This includes: non-provisional U.S. applications in which the agency or lab has an ownership interest; non-provisional applications where the invention is owned jointly with another party, regardless of which party is filing the application; and applications such as continuations, continuations in part and divisional applications. This number does not include provisional applications or any application filed under the authority of the Patent Cooperation Treaty (PCT). PCT applications are not included in the metric "Patent Applications Filed" because they do not result in patents.

Table 5.2 shows the number of new licenses over the fiscal years FY2003 through FY2019. As also defined in the DOC's *Guidance for Preparing Annual Agency Technology Transfer Reports* (2020, p. 9), a license is:

> ... a written contract between the owner/licensor of a patent, copyright, trademark, know-how, service mark, or other intellectual property, and a licensee to use, manufacture, or sell copies of the original. Commercialization of a technology is a major purpose for licensing agreements. These contracts typically (1) limit the licensee's scope or field, (2) make the license exclusive or nonexclusive, (3) demands royalties or other compensation if further licensing occurs by the licensee. The government may grant non-exclusive, partially exclusive, or exclusive licenses.

Table 5.3 shows the number of new invention licenses over the fiscal years FY2003 through FY2019. As defined in the DOC's *Guidance for Preparing Annual Agency Technology Transfer Reports* (2020, p. 9), an invention license is:

> [a license that] includes patents, biological materials, plant varieties, or tangible materials. It can be income bearing or non-income bearing.

Table 5.4 shows the number of new CRADAs (traditional and other CRADAs) over the fiscal years FY2003 through FY2019. And finally, as defined in the DOC's *Guidance for Preparing Annual Agency Technology Transfer Reports* (2020, p. 7):

> [A CRADA is] an agreement that is executed under the authority of 15 USC 3710a[4] and that includes a Research Plan or Statement of Work.

Table 5.1   *Data on patent applications filed with the U.S. Patent and Trademark Office, by agency and by fiscal year FY2003–FY2019*

Agency	FY2003	FY2004	FY2005	FY2006	FY2007	FY2008	FY2009	FY2010	FY2011	FY2012	FY2013	FY2014	FY2015	FY2016	FY2017	FY2018	FY2019
USDA	60	81	88	83	114	123	123	113	124	122	157	119	125	109	111	120	97
DOC	5	12	12	5	8	21	20	20	17	27	26	25	32	25	46	56	65
DOD	810	517	354	691	597	590	690	436	844	1013	942	898	875	858	869	1,060	955
DOE	866	661	812	726	693	904	775	1,051	1,060	933	944	1,144	949	999	937	868	837
HHS	279	216	230	166	261	164	284	291	272	233	230	216	222	269	289	253	207
DHS	–	–	–	–	0	0	2	2	12	10	4	6	12	15	0	17	38
DOI	8	6	3	2	5	7	8	7	2	3	8	4	8	4	5	7	3
DOT	0	2	5	3	2	2	2	2	2	1	5	0	5	0	7	0	2
VA	36	54	26	27	25	13	37	13	29	94	106	116	116	104	163	255	274
EPA	23	12	13	13	15	6	3	3	8	10	7	9	4	1	4	6	6
NASA	231	207	209	142	127	122	141	150	128	130	150	140	129	129	165	144	85
TOTAL	2,318	1,768	1,752	1,858	1,847	1,952	2,085	2,088	2,498	2,576	2,579	2,677	2,477	2,513	2,596	2,786	2,569

Note: USDA refers to the U.S. Department of Agriculture, DOC refers to the U.S. Department of Commerce, DOD refers to the U.S. Department of Defense, DOE refers to the U.S. Department of Energy, HHS refers to the U.S. Department of Health and Human Services, DHS refers to the U.S. Department of Homeland Security, DOI refers to the U.S. Department of the Interior, DOT refers to the U.S. Department of Transportation, VA refers to the U.S. Department of Veteran Affairs, EPA refers to the U.S. Environmental Protection Agency, NASA refers to the U.S. National Aeronautics and Space Administration. A dash (–) indicates that the data were either unavailable, not collected for, or not reported for the Federal Technology Transfer Report in the current or proceeding fiscal years.
Prior to FY2003, the technology transfer data were reported with various, different metrics. This resulted in large gaps in the database for those metrics that were reported differently in prior fiscal year reports.
Source: https://www.nist.gov/tpo/reports-and-publications, accessed January 4, 2023.

Table 5.2   *Data on new licenses, by agency and by fiscal year FY2003–FY2019*

Agency	FY2003	FY2004	FY2005	FY2006	FY2007	FY2008	FY2009	FY2010	FY2011	FY2012	FY2013	FY2014	FY2015	FY2016	FY2017	FY2018	FY2019
USDA	27	29	33	25	25	28	26	22	35	34	25	31	37	31	38	41	51
DOC	59	100	108	83	187	2	12	7	5	6	7	7	13	15	19	11	15
DOD	49	60	60	56	67	52	57	50	63	44	59	24	69	35	162	168	58
DOE	711	616	750	652	606	685	755	826	822	757	568	573	648	621	567	662	686
HHS	230	288	349	290	293	277	221	269	264	231	184	212	279	278	334	335	346
DHS	–	–	–	–	–	0	45	458	0	0	0	3	3	1	0	0	0
DOI	1	3	5	1	1	1	4	4	2	3	0	0	3	0	0	2	2
DOT	0	0	4	0	0	0	0	0	1	1	1	0	0	2	1	1	0
VA	7	9	6	11	18	23	10	6	11	8	9	3	3	1	1	n.a.	n.a.
EPA	9	7	4	2	5	2	3	2	6	2	2	6	0	8	5	1	3
NASA	270	423	506	655	721	633	803	498	30	33	38	51	74	107	119	105	96
TOTAL	1,363	1,535	1,825	1,775	1,923	1,703	1,936	2,142	1,239	1,116	896	907	1,129	1,099	1,246	1,326	1,257

Note: USDA refers to the U.S. Department of Agriculture, DOC refers to the U.S. Department of Commerce, DOD refers to the U.S. Department of Defense, DOE refers to the U.S. Department of Energy, HHS refers to the U.S. Department of Health and Human Services, DHS refers to the U.S. Department of Homeland Security, DOI refers to the U.S. Department of the Interior, DOT refers to the U.S. Department of Transportation, VA refers to the U.S. Department of Veteran Affairs, EPA refers to the U.S. Environmental Protection Agency, NASA refmers to the U.S. National Aeronautics and Space Administration. A dash (–) indicates that the data were either unavailable, not collected for, or not reported for the Federal Technology Transfer Report in the current or proceeding fiscal years.

Prior to FY2003, the technology transfer data were reported with various, different metrics. This resulted in large gaps in the database for those metrics that were reported differently in prior fiscal year reports. n.a. means "not available."

Source: https://www.nist.gov/tpo/reports-and-publications, accessed January 4, 2023.

Table 5.3 Data on new invention licenses, by agency and by fiscal year FY2003–FY2019

Agency	FY2003	FY2004	FY2005	FY2006	FY2007	FY2008	FY2009	FY2010	FY2011	FY2012	FY2013	FY2014	FY2015	FY2016	FY2017	FY2018	FY2019
USDA	27	29	33	25	25	24	22	18	29	28	19	29	22	25	31	27	17
DOC	59	100	108	83	187	2	11	7	5	6	7	7	13	15	19	11	15
DOD	49	60	60	56	67	52	57	50	63	44	59	6	69	57	24	n.a.	58
DOE	172	168	198	203	164	177	139	166	169	192	153	171	155	145	128	100	98
HHS	218	249	291	253	234	233	198	217	106	192	152	117	232	221	282	292	291
DHS	–	–	–	–	–	0	0	0	0	0	0	0	3	1	0	0	0
DOI	1	3	5	1	0	1	3	3	2	1	3	0	3	0	0	n.a.	2
DOT	0	0	4	4	0	0	0	0	0	0	1	0	0	0	0	0	0
VA	7	9	6	11	18	23	10	6	11	8	9	3	3	1	0	n.a.	n.a.
EPA	9	7	4	2	5	2	3	2	6	2	2	6	0	8	5	1	3
NASA	71	107	130	47	45	34	49	36	20	28	31	45	69	97	109	99	88
TOTAL	613	732	839	685	745	548	492	505	411	501	436	384	569	570	598	530	572

Note: USDA refers to the U.S. Department of Agriculture, DOC refers to the U.S. Department of Commerce, DOD refers to the U.S. Department of Defense, DOE refers to the U.S. Department of Energy, HHS refers to the U.S. Department of Health and Human Services, DHS refers to the U.S. Department of Homeland Security, DOI refers to the U.S. Department of the Interior, DOT refers to the U.S. Department of Transportation, VA refers to the U.S. Department of Veteran Affairs, EPA refers to the U.S. Environmental Protection Agency, NASA refers to the U.S. National Aeronautics and Space Administration. A dash (–) indicates that the data were either unavailable, not collected for, or not reported for the Federal Technology Transfer Report in the current or preceding fiscal years.
Prior to FY2003, the technology transfer data were reported with various, different metrics. This resulted in large gaps in the database for those metrics that were reported differently in prior fiscal year reports. n.a. means "not available."
Source: https://www.nist.gov/tpo/reports-and-publications, accessed January 4, 2023.

Table 5.4   *Data on new CRADAs, by agency and by fiscal year FY2003–FY2019*

Agency	FY2003	FY2004	FY2005	FY2006	FY2007	FY2008	FY2009	FY2010	FY2011	FY2012	FY2013	FY2014	FY2015	FY2016	FY2017	FY2018	FY2019
USDA	55	44	55	57	69	77	81	92	102	65	86	60	80	79	91	61	95
DOC	1,767	1,790	1,764	2,158	1,865	1,585	1,512	2,159	2,192	2,323	2,289	2,111	2,548	2,608	2,443	2,770	1,893
DOD	630	768	679	705	641	745	659	720	762	757	769	686	786	774	813	949	936
DOE	140	157	164	168	182	178	176	176	208	184	142	174	186	264	330	312	287
HHS	102	95	101	66	68	83	105	83	81	93	104	98	112	134	112	87	93
DHS	–	–	–	–	–	8	6	14	31	53	76	88	98	114	107	104	60
DOI	12	16	21	38	112	98	74	82	295	284	376	423	586	511	477	422	352
DOT	7	0	5	6	7	6	7	0	8	12	8	10	9	22	6	7	10
VA	8	4	3	26	52	155	438	491	450	542	453	517	509	502	575	512	536
EPA	39	23	33	16	18	49	83	33	26	22	51	35	23	14	8	11	11
NASA	0	0	1	0	0	0	1	0	0	0	0	1	7	5	0	0	0
TOTAL	2,760	2,897	2,826	3,240	3,014	2,984	3,142	3,850	4,155	4,335	4,354	4,203	4,944	5,027	4,962	5,235	4,273

Note: USDA refers to the U.S. Department of Agriculture, DOC refers to the U.S. Department of Commerce, DOD refers to the U.S. Department of Defense, DOE refers to the U.S. Department of Energy, HHS refers to the U.S. Department of Health and Human Services, DHS refers to the U.S. Department of Homeland Security, DOI refers to the U.S. Department of the Interior, DOT refers to the U.S. Department of Transportation, VA refers to the U.S. Department of Veteran Affairs, EPA refers to the U.S. Environmental Protection Agency, NASA refers to the U.S. National Aeronautics and Space Administration. A dash (–) indicates that the data were either unavailable, not collected for, or not reported for the Federal Technology Transfer Report in the current or proceeding fiscal years.
Prior to FY2003, the technology transfer data were reported with various, different metrics. This resulted in large gaps in the database for those metrics that were reported differently in prior fiscal year reports.
Source: https://www.nist.gov/tpo/reports-and-publications, accessed January 4, 2023.

As described in more detail in USDOC (2019, p. 11), collaborative research is:

> Collaborative R&D relationships between federal laboratories and non-federal collaborators are widely viewed as an effective and economical means of transferring technology through joint research. These relationships create a mutually advantageous leveraging of federal agency and collaborator resources and technical capabilities. They also provide avenues for both the collaborator and the federal laboratory to gain new competencies and develop new skills.
>
> One frequently used mechanism for establishing joint research relationships is the cooperative research and development agreement (CRADA). The CRADA is a multifaceted mechanism that can be used to address several kinds of partnership needs. "Traditional CRADAs" refer to formal collaborative R&D agreements between a federal laboratory and nonfederal partners. Other special CRADA arrangements are used by federal agencies to address special purpose applications such as material transfer agreements or agreements that facilitate technical assistance activities.

Using the agency totals in Tables 5.1 through 5.4, I describe here the trend in the four technology transfer metrics that are illustrated in Figures 5.1 through 5.4 without any attribution to causal economic events. The trend in patent applications is shown in Figure 5.1, the trend in new licenses is shown in Figure 5.2, the trend in new invention licenses is shown in Figure 5.3, and the trend in new CRADAs is shown in Figure 5.4.

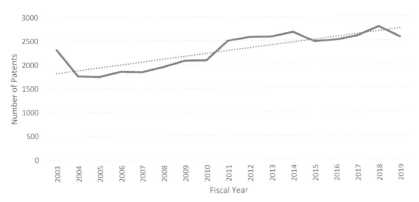

Note: The dotted line is an Excel-generated trend line.
Source: Table 5.1.

Figure 5.1   *Trend in patent applications filed with the U.S. Patent and Trademark Office (USPTO), all agencies by fiscal year FY2003–FY2019*

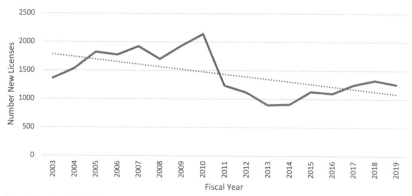

Note: The dotted line is an Excel-generated trend line.
Source: Table 5.2.

Figure 5.2   *Trend in new licenses, all agencies by fiscal year*
                 FY2003–FY2019

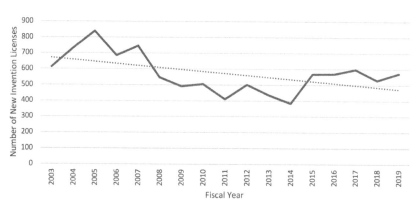

Note: The dotted line is an Excel-generated trend line.
Source: Table 5.3.

Figure 5.3   *Trend in new invention licenses, all agencies by fiscal year*
                 FY2003–FY2019

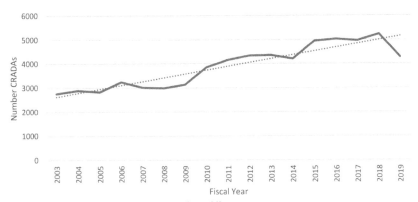

Note: The dotted line is an Excel-generated trend line.
Source: Table 5.4.

Figure 5.4   *Trend in new CRADAs, all agencies by fiscal year*
              FY2003–FY2019

Imposed on each of these four figures is a generated trend line. The trend in patent applications and new CRADAS is positive, and it appears to be relatively smooth over the fiscal years shown. The trend in licenses and new invention licenses is negative, and the trend in new invention licenses over the period of the Great Recession appears to be below the overall trend.

SELECTED TRENDS IN TECHNOLOGY TRANSFER METRICS

In this section, I describe visually trends in four technology transfer metrics in three agencies. The four technology transfer metrics illustrated above are patent applications, new licenses, new invention licenses, and new CRADAS. The figures below are specific to Department of Defense (DOD), Department of Energy (DOE), and National Aeronautics and Space Administration (NASA); these are among the larger federal agencies that engage in R&D (and to anticipate what follows, these are the agencies for which disaggregate R&D investment data are available). Also, these figures show each technology transfer metric denominated by total R&D (Table 5.5) and by the total number of U.S. STEM employees (Table 5.6).

Table 5.5   *Data on total R&D (millions $2022), by selected agency and by fiscal year FY2003–FY2019*

Fiscal Year	DOD	DOE	NASA	TOTAL (all departments and all agencies)
FY2003	$88,172	$12,571	$15,883	$175,643
FY2004	$95,769	$12,652	$15,688	$183,440
FY2005	$99,022	$12,146	$14,963	$185,037
FY2006	$101,441	$11,721	$15,423	$185,791
FY2007	$105,024	$12,009	$15,396	$188,668
FY2008	$105,708	$12,723	$14,565	$188,122
FY2009	$104,908	$13,262	$11,314	$187,463
FY2010	$105,824	$13,832	$11,823	$190,958
FY2011	$99,011	$13,358	$11,387	$180,680
FY2012	$91,456	$13,279	$13,898	$175,052
FY2013	$79,046	$12,910	$13,266	$158,575
FY2014	$78,693	$14,192	$13,907	$161,596
FY2015	$77,816	$16,827	$13,350	$161,811
FY2016	$84,413	$17,401	$15,390	$173,073
FY2017	$57,390	$17,453	$12,195	$145,070
FY2018	$68,768	$19,418	$12,342	$160,724
FY2019	$70,647	$19,955	$11,684	$163,799

Note: DOD refers to the U.S. Department of Defense, DOE refers to the U.S. Department of Energy, NASA refers to the U.S. National Aeronautics and Space Administration. Beginning in FY2017, federal agencies have revised what they consider to be R&D. Late-stage development, testing, and evaluation programs, primarily within the DOD, are no longer counted as R&D. This was reversed in FY2019.
Source: https://www.aaas.org/programs/r-d-budget-and-policy/historical-trends-federal-rd, accessed January 4, 2023.

Table 5.6   Data on number of U.S. science, technology, engineering, and mathematics (STEM) employees, by selected agency and by fiscal year FY2003–FY2019

Fiscal Year	DOD	DOE	NASA	TOTAL (all departments and all agencies)
FY2003	6,464	4,932	10,998	211,601
FY2004	8,993	4,880	11,017	231,405
FY2005	8,627	4,747	11,355	234,668
FY2006	8,768	4,663	11,173	236,461
FY2007	8,662	4,562	11,109	238,574
FY2008	8,962	4,502	11,244	238,174
FY2009	9,042	4,634	11,485	242,298
FY2010	9,640	4,763	11,555	254,767
FY2011	10,701	4,928	11,751	267,877
FY2012	11,171	4,877	11,821	272,193
FY2013	11,571	4,731	11,594	270,848
FY2014	11,759	4,629	11,564	267,383
FY2015	13,099	5,002	11,516	315,037
FY2016	13,053	5,041	11,298	319,294
FY2017	13,468	5,082	11,247	324,704
FY2018	13,413	5,008	11,359	325,543
FY2019	13,431	4,880	11,428	326,750

Note: DOD refers to the U.S. Department of Defense, DOE refers to the U.S. Department of Energy, NASA refers to the U.S. National Aeronautics and Space Administration. Reported in the table are the number of U.S. STEM employees at the beginning of each fiscal year.
Source: https://www.fedscope.opm.gov/employment.asp, accessed January 5, 2023.

Figures 5.5 through 5.7 show the trend in denominated patent applications for DOD, DOE, and NASA, respectively. The data for these figures come from the tables above. Visually, I think that one would be hard pressed to conclude from the DOE and NASA figures that patent applications per R&D investments or per STEM employees declined during the Great Recession. The visual trend during the Great Recession for DOD is unclear; a point that is revisited in the following section.

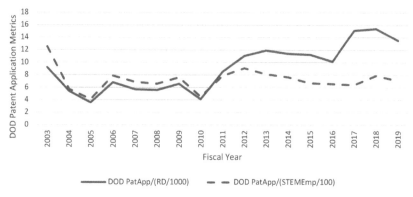

Figure 5.5   *Trend in patent application metrics for DOD, by fiscal year FY2003–FY2019*

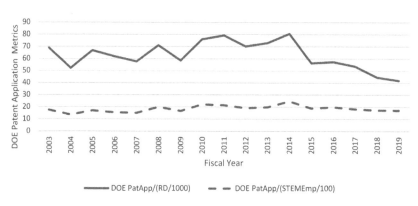

Figure 5.6   *Trend in patent application metrics for DOE, by fiscal year FY2003–FY2019*

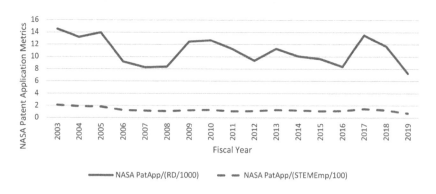

Figure 5.7   *Trend in patent application metrics for NASA, by fiscal year FY2003–FY2019*

Figures 5.8 through 5.10 show the trend in denominated new licenses for DOD, DOE, and NASA, respectively. The data for these figures come from the tables above. Visually, there appears to be a decline in denominated metrics for DOE a few years after the Great Recession and for NASA only shortly after the Great Recession.

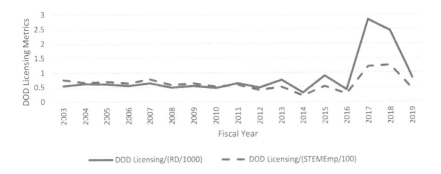

Figure 5.8   *Trend in new license metrics for DOD, by fiscal year FY2003–FY2019*

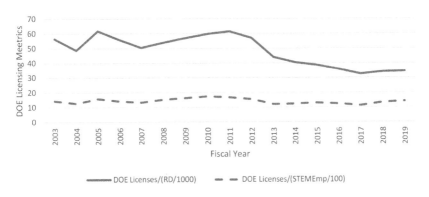

Figure 5.9   *Trend in new license metrics for DOE, by fiscal year FY2003–FY2019*

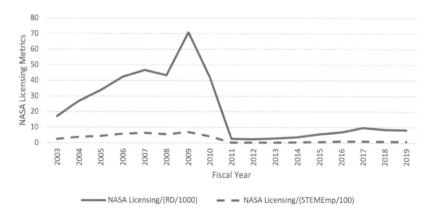

Figure 5.10   Trend in new license metrics for NASA, by fiscal year FY2003–FY2019

Figures 5.11 through 5.13 show the trend in denominated new invention licenses for DOD, DOE, and NASA, respectively. The data for these figures come from the tables above. Visually, the impact of the Great Recession on these metrics is unclear. For example, one might interpret the decline in new licenses per R&D among the three agencies as having begun before the Great Recession, which is especially evident for NASA.

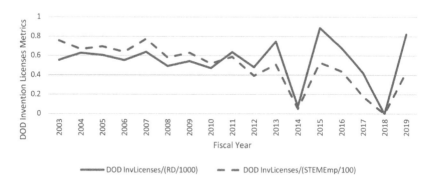

Figure 5.11   Trend in new invention license metrics for DOD, by fiscal year FY2003–FY2019

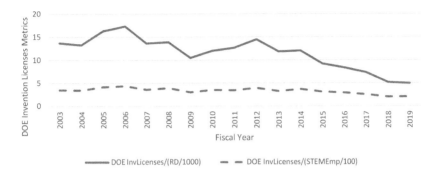

*Figure 5.12   Trend in new invention license metrics for DOE, by fiscal
year FY2003–FY2019*

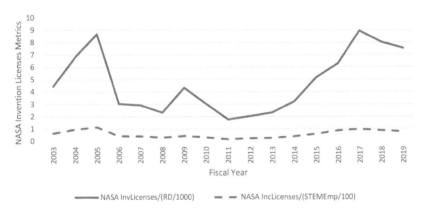

*Figure 5.13   Trend in new invention license metrics for NASA, by fiscal
year FY2003–FY2019*

And Figures 5.14 and 5.15 show the trend in denominated new CRADAs for
DOD and DOE, respectively. Note in Table 5.4 that NASA rarely engages
in technology transfers through CRADAs. The data for these figures come
from the tables above. Visually, it is unclear if a definitive relationship existed
during the Great Recession.

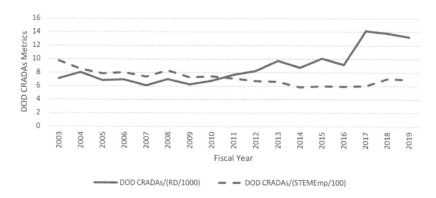

*Figure 5.14   Trend in new CRADA metrics for DOD, by fiscal year
           FY2003–FY2019*

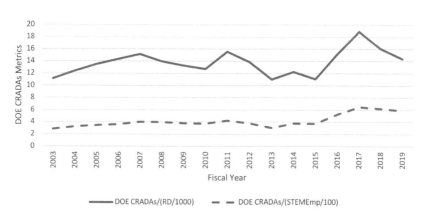

*Figure 5.15   Trend in new CRADA metrics for DOE, by fiscal year
           FY2003–FY2019*

To summarize, overall, I would not generalize from the above visuals, with the possible exception of new licenses at NASA (see Figure 5.10) that the Great Recession affected any of these technology transfer metrics.

INPUT CORRELATES AND COVARIATES WITH TECHNOLOGY TRANSFER OUTPUTS

In this section, I describe the statistical relationship between alternative research capital resources (defined below) in a federal laboratory and the technology transfer outputs associated with those resources.

Specifically, I present in Table 5.9 the simple correlation coefficients associated with three research capital inputs—total investment in R&D (*R&D*), investments in research (*Research*), and investments in basic research (*Basic*). The variable *Research* was constructed as the sum of investments in basic research (Table 5.7) and applied research (Table 5.8), respectively—and the four technology transfer mechanisms previously discussed.

Table 5.7 *Data on basic research (millions $2022), by selected agency and by fiscal year FY2003–FY2019*

Fiscal Year	DOD	DOE	NASA	TOTAL (all departments and all agencies)
FY2003	$2,035.10	$3,800.60	$3,281.00	$37,655.50
FY2004	$1,972.10	$3,952.60	$3,591.90	$38,524.20
FY2005	$2,092.00	$4,039.90	$3,502.80	$39,003.70
FY2006	$1,989.90	$4,001.00	$3,139.30	$37,326.90
FY2007	$2,026.80	$4,165.80	$3,081.80	$37,439.60
FY2008	$2,071.60	$4,507.40	$2,842.50	$37,429.30
FY2009	$2,250.20	$4,886.00	$1,158.70	$36,256.30
FY2010	$2,316.40	$5,068.90	$1,065.90	$37,423.00
FY2011	$2,348.90	$4,979.80	$1,498.00	$37,296.30
FY2012	$2,468.90	$4,804.90	$3,907.10	$39,065.40
FY2013	$2,293.20	$4,644.50	$3,557.60	$36,425.90
FY2014	$2,489.20	$4,840.30	$3,928.20	$37,967.30
FY2015	$2,589.30	$5,236.50	$3,754.90	$37,325.60
FY2016	$2,586.10	$5,339.80	$4,149.00	$38,162.30
FY2017	$2,511.10	$5,190.90	$4,108.70	$38,815.30
FY2018	$2,527.30	$5,571.10	$3,653.40	$40,312.30
FY2019	$2,709.30	$5,619.50	$5,404.10	$42,978.60

Note: DOD refers to the U.S. Department of Defense, DOE refers to the U.S. Department of Energy, NASA refers to the U.S. National Aeronautics and Space Administration. Beginning in FY2017, federal agencies have revised what they consider to be R&D. Late-stage development, testing, and evaluation programs, primarily within the DOD, are no longer counted as R&D. This was reversed in FY2019.
Source: https://www.aaas.org/programs/r-d-budget-and-policy/historical-trends-federal-rd, accessed January 5, 2023.

Table 5.8   *Data on applied research (millions $2022), by selected*
                     agency and by fiscal year FY2003–FY2019

Fiscal Year	DOD	DOE	NASA	TOTAL (all departments and all agencies)
FY2003	$7,027.90	$3,993.20	$4,741.40	$40,841.60
FY2004	$7,019.50	$4,006.60	$4,365.20	$41,818.30
FY2005	$7,483.50	$4,074.00	$3,082.40	$40,658.30
FY2006	$7,529.60	$3,673.20	$2,294.00	$38,655.80
FY2007	$7,686.80	$4,006.50	$1,377.00	$38,015.40
FY2008	$7,486.30	$4,141.40	$731.20	$36,601.20
FY2009	$7,553.20	$3,875.30	$901.30	$38,870.00
FY2010	$8,653.40	$4,349.00	$833.60	$40,587.70
FY2011	$7,417.90	$4,474.20	$2,932.40	$40,581.50
FY2012	$7,877.30	$4,402.00	$3,254.80	$40,933.00
FY2013	$7,148.00	$4,647.90	$3,277.00	$39,760.20
FY2014	$8,186.40	$5,382.30	$2,889.60	$41,165.40
FY2015	$8,066.10	$6,551.20	$2,725.50	$42,229.30
FY2016	$8,964.80	$7,398.50	$2,828.40	$42,955.60
FY2017	$8,905.80	$7,615.30	$2,821.10	$46,290.60
FY2018	$9,442.40	$8,873.70	$2,239.10	$48,347.20
FY2019	$9,711.60	$9,012.60	$2,995.80	$49,903.60

Note: DOD refers to the U.S. Department of Defense, DOE refers to the U.S. Department of Energy, NASA refers to the U.S. National Aeronautics and Space Administration. Beginning in FY2017, federal agencies have revised what they consider to be R&D. Late-stage development, testing, and evaluation programs, primarily within the DOD, are no longer counted as R&D. This was reversed in FY2019.
Source: https://www.aaas.org/programs/r-d-budget-and-policy/historical-trends-federal-rd, accessed January 5, 2023.

Consider the following National Science Foundation's definitions:[5]

Conduct of research and development (R&D): Research and experimental development activities are defined as creative and systematic work undertaken in order to increase the stock of knowledge—including knowledge of people, culture, and society—and to devise new applications using available knowledge.

Basic research is defined as experimental or theoretical work undertaken primarily to acquire new knowledge of underlying foundations of phenomena and observable facts. Basic research may include activities with broad or general applications in mind, such as the study of how plant genomes change, but should exclude research directed towards a specific application or requirement include, such as the optimization of the genome of a specific crop species.

Applied research is defined as original investigation undertaken in order to acquire new knowledge. Applied research is, however, directed primarily towards a specific practical aim or objective.

Experimental development is defined as creative and systematic work, drawing on knowledge gained from research and practical experience, which is directed at producing new products or processes or improving existing products or processes. Like research, experimental development will result in gaining additional knowledge.

One might expect there to be a positive correlation among these research capital variables and the technology transfer metrics discussed above. The results of the research activity, measured in terms of the laboratory's access to research capital resources, in an agency's laboratory might reasonably be, among other things, the implementation of technology transfer mechanisms (quantified in Tables 5.1 through 5.4).

There are caveats associated with my proposed so-called *research capital resource to technology transfer mechanism relationship*. First, research activity can be measured in several ways. There is, of course, the total amount of investments in R&D. However, it is not intuitive that laboratory investments in development—the D in R&D—are the most appropriate input to associate with all or some of the technology transfer metrics discussed above. What might be the more appropriate input is laboratory investments in research—the R in R&D. For DOD, DOE, and NASA, data are available on investments in basic research and in applied research; the sum of investments in basic research and applied research equals the laboratory's investments in research.

Second, there is likely a lag involved in the process from the use of research capital resources and the realization of technology to be transferred. In all likelihood, such a lag will vary across the three measures of research resources with the lag between investments in basic research and any resulting technology transfer metrics perhaps being the longest. And the lag will vary across departments and agency because the nature of their research varies.

Third, contemporary investments in research capital might have a lesser impact in generating the use of contemporary technology transfer metrics than the accumulated stock (built over several years) of research capital investments.

Fourth, research resources are not the only resources used in the process of generating new technology transfer metrics. Human resources are also involved, but how one precisely or accurately measures the amount of human resources associated with departmental or agency research is unknown. Counting the total number of employees in a department or agency probably overstates the level of related human resources. What might be the more appropriate input to laboratory investments in R&D or research is the number of STEM (science, technology, engineering, and mathematics) employees (see Table 5.6 above), but even counting the number of STEM employees does not account for quality differences among individuals.

And fifth, if one were to develop a model to estimate an agency's laboratory across-year variation in the number of new technology transfer mechanisms, one would want to hold constant relevant research resources as well as human resources in the same way that one would estimate a production function between physical capital (K), labor (L), and output (Q): $Q = f(K, L)$. However, the available measure of research resources—R&D, R, and basic research— are not independent of the measure of human resources because the latter are funded through the former investments.

Table 5.9 shows the correlation coefficients between investments in research resources and contemporary technology transfer measures. These metrics are a second-order approximation of this relationship due to the caveats discussed above. Nevertheless, there are several takeaways from the patterns in Table 5.9 that might serve researchers well as future efforts are undertaken to identify a relevant framework for modeling the research resource inputs to technology transfer output relationship.

The first generalization from the correlation coefficients in Table 5.9 is that for DOD, contemporary R&D investments are not positive and significant correlates except for with new invention licenses. Investments in research and in basic research are positive and significant correlates with new patent applications and CRADAs. Also, the applied nature of research capital appears to influence research collaborations more than the basic nature of research capital as evidenced by a larger correlation coefficient for *DODResearch* than for *DODBasic*, but the reverse is true for patent applications.

For DOE, it appears that contemporary investments in basic research are positive and significant correlates with patent applications, and all categories of research capital are positive and significantly correlated with new CRADAs; the correlation coefficients for research capital are greatest for total R&D and least for basic research. Perhaps the development aspect of total investments in R&D is important for demonstrating to potential collaborative research partners that the research at DOE has verified market applicability. The applied nature of research capital appears to influence research collaborations more than the basic nature of research capital as evidenced by a larger correlation coefficient for *DOEResearch* than for *DOEBasic*.

Finally, for NASA, the relationship between patent applications and total investments in R&D is positive and significant, as is the relationship between invention licenses and both investments in research and also in basic research.

Table 5.9   Research-related correlates with DOD, DOE, and NASA technology transfer metrics

Variable	DODRD	DODResearch	DODBasic	DOERD	DOEResearch	DOEBasic	NASARD	NASAResearch	NASABasic
DODPatApps	-0.713***	0.495**	0.695***	–	–	–	–	–	–
DOEPatApps	–	–	–	0.246	0.308	0.517**	–	–	–
NASAPatApps	-0.569**	–	–	–	–	–	0.465*	0.247	-0.104
DODLicenses	–	0.400	0.228	–	–	–	–	–	–
DOELicenses	–	–	–	-0.205	-0.233	0.027	–	–	–
NASALicenses	–	–	–	–	–	–	0.249	-0.615***	-0.510**
DODInvLicenses	0.438*	-0.270	-0.268	–	–	–	–	–	–
DOEInvLicenses	–	–	–	-0.857***	-0.846***	-0.748***	–	–	–
NASAInvLicenses	–	–	–	–	–	–	0.203	0.505**	0.505**
DODCRADAs	-0.663***	0.738***	0.667***	–	–	–	–	–	–
DOECRADAs	–	–	–	0.866***	0.882***	0.743***	–	–	–

Note: *** significant at .01-level or better, ** significant at .05-level, * significant at .10-level.
Key: *PatApps* refers to patent applications, *Licenses* refers to new licenses, *InvLicenses* refers to new invention licenses, *CRADAs* refers to new CRADAs.

INVENTION DISCLOSURES AS A KNOWLEDGE TRANSFER

In Chapter 2 and in the opening sentence to this chapter, I wrote that the so-called mirepoix of technology transfer channels or mechanisms includes patents, licenses, and collaborative research efforts. Each of these technology transfer mechanisms has been discussed and illustrated above. In addition to research resources being devoted to the so-called production of these outputs, as inferred from the discussion of the correlates in Table 5.9, there are also human resources that are associated with these outputs. One aspect of human resources is the knowledge base that is so embodied. And a mechanism that might reasonably approximate the manifestation of this knowledge base is invention disclosures. In Chapter 2, I noted that there is a literature in economics and management that has focused on the creative response of firms to the Great Recession. From Table 5.10 the total number of new invention disclosures increased uniformly in the two fiscal years after the Great Recession. For FY2008 through FY2010, the number of new invention disclosures was 7,777, 7,937, and 8,488, respectively. For FY2011 and FY2013, the number of new invention disclosures increased to 9,367 and 10,248.

As defined in the DOC's *Guidance for Preparing Annual Agency Technology Transfer Reports* (2020, p. 8):

> Invention: Any art or process, machine, manufacture, design, or composition of matter, or any new and useful improvement thereof, or any variety of plant, which is or may be patentable under the patent laws of the United States.

> Invention Disclosures: Federal employees are required to report inventions in a reasonable time though the agency's Invention Disclosure Form. The number of Invention Disclosures refers to the number of invention disclosure forms submitted to an agency's management during the fiscal year.

In this section, I explore how the knowledge transfer mechanism of invention disclosures is related to one of the four technology transfer mechanisms, namely, to patent applications.[6] For the estimation of new invention disclosures (*InvDisc*) on new patent applications (*PatApps*), I considered a model in which supporting resources are held constant. As discussed above, research resources are one supporting resource and human resources are a second supporting resource. Research resources can take the aggregate form of investments in R&D (*R&D*), or they can be more focused and take the form of investments in basic and applied research (*Research*) or even investments in basic research (*Basic*). Human resources take the form of STEM employees (*Emp*). The model below does not consider both research and human resources as having

Table 5.10   Data on new invention disclosures, by agency and by fiscal year FY2003–FY2019

Agency	FY2003	FY2004	FY2005	FY2006	FY2007	FY2008	FY2009	FY2010	FY2011	FY2012	FY2013	FY2014	FY2015	FY2016	FY2017	FY2018	FY2019
USDA	121	142	125	105	126	100	178	149	158	160	191	117	222	244	166	320	243
DOC	21	25	21	14	32	40	40	31	26	60	41	47	61	64	43	77	60
DOD	1,332	1,369	534	1,056	838	1,018	831	698	929	1,078	1,032	902	743	782	978	839	839
DOE	1,469	1,617	1,776	1,694	1,575	1,460	1,439	1,616	1,820	1,661	1,796	1,588	1,645	1,760	1,794	1,748	1,891
HHS	472	461	452	442	447	437	353	337	351	352	320	351	321	320	354	322	268
DHS	–	–	–	–	10	10	32	7	38	40	21	44	12	15	20	22	14
DOI	9	6	4	5	7	7	4	5	5	10	9	6	7	8	12	9	8
DOT	0	0	4	3	2	3	3	1	2	2	13	3	0	0	3	12	2
VA	183	204	165	157	175	164	150	171	191	310	282	289	219	241	589	496	724
EPA	14	18	12	12	16	9	8	5	8	18	8	5	7	6	13	7	6
NASA	1,485	1,612	1,682	1,749	1,514	1,324	1,412	1,735	1,748	1,656	1,627	1,701	1,550	1,554	1,690	1,775	1,841
TOTAL	9,055	8,613	7,545	8,320	7,970	7,777	7,937	8,488	9,367	10,248	9,966	9,923	9,447	9,807	10,533	10,799	11,065

Note: USDA refers to the U.S. Department of Agriculture, DOC refers to the U.S. Department of Commerce, DOD refers to the U.S. Department of Defense, DOE refers to the U.S. Department of Energy, HHS refers to the U.S. Department of Health and Human Services, DHS refers to the U.S. Department of Homeland Security, DOI refers to the U.S. Department of the Interior, DOT refers to the U.S. Department of Transportation, VA refers to the U.S. Department of Veteran Affairs, EPA refers to the U.S. Environmental Protection Agency, NASA refers to the U.S. National Aeronautics and Space Administration. A dash (–) indicates that the data were either unavailable, not collected for, or not reported for the Federal Technology Transfer Report in the current or preceding fiscal years. Prior to FY2003, the technology transfer data were reported with various, different metrics. This resulted in large gaps in the database for those metrics that were reported differently in prior fiscal year reports.

Source: https://www.nist.gov/tpo/reports-and-publications, accessed January 5, 2023.

independent effects on patent applications because investments in research resources include the cost of attendant employees as also discussed above.[7]

Thus, consider the following Cobb-Douglas production models:[8]

$$PatApps = A\ Emp^{\alpha}\ InvDisc^{\beta} \tag{5.1}$$

$$PatApps = A\ R\&D^{\alpha}\ InvDisc^{\beta} \tag{5.2}$$

$$PatApps = A\ Reseach^{\alpha}\ InvDisc^{\beta} \tag{5.3}$$

$$PatApps = A\ Basic^{\alpha}\ InvDisc^{\beta} \tag{5.4}$$

Taking logarithms of both sides of each of the above equations yields:[9,10]

$$\log (PatApps) = \log (A) + (\alpha + \beta) \log (Emp) + \beta \log (InvDisc/Emp) + \varepsilon \tag{5.5}$$

$$\log (PatApps) = \log (A) + (\alpha + \beta) \log (R\&D) + \beta \log (InvDisc/R\&D) + \varepsilon \tag{5.6}$$

$$\log (PatApps) = \log (A) + (\alpha + \beta) \log (Research) + \beta \log (InvDisc/Research) + \varepsilon \tag{5.7}$$

$$\log (PatApps) = \log (A) + (\alpha + \beta) \log (Basic) + \beta \log (InvDisc/Basic) + \varepsilon \tag{5.8}$$

where A is a disembodied shift factor and the parameters α and β vary across equations. As above, data on *R&D*, *Research*, and *Basic* are only available for DOD, DOE, and NASA. The observations from DOD, DOE, and NASA are aggregated (n = 51) to achieve a greater number of observations for implementing the above regression models. Fixed agency effects are held constant (*DeptDOD* and *DeptDOE*) along with a binary variable to account for the Great Recession (*GR*).[11]

The least-squares regression results from the estimation of equations (5.5) through (5.8) are in Table 5.11. Of particular interest is $\beta > 0$ because it represents the denominated invention disclosures elasticity of new patent applications. In other words, a 1 percent increase in denominated invention disclosures is associated with a β percent increase in new patent applications.

Table 5.11   *Least-squares regression results from equations (5.5) through (5.8) (n = 51) (standard errors in parentheses)*

Dependent Variable	Estimating Equations							
	(1)	(2)	(3)	(4)	(5)	(6)	(7)	(8)
	Eq. (5.5)	Eq. (5.6)	Eq. (5.7)	Eq. (5.8)	Eq. (5.5)	Eq. (5.6)	Eq. (5.7)	Eq. (5.8)
log (*Emp*)	1.284*** (0.365)	–	–	–	1.264*** (0.389)	–	–	–
log (*InvDisc/ Emp*)	0.487*** (0.199)	–			0.478** (0.210)	–		
log (*R&D*)	–	0.220 (0.338)	–	–	–	0.208 (0.339)	–	–
log (*InvDisc/R&D*)	–	0.434** (0.184)	–	–	–	0.417** (0.191)	–	–
log (*Research*)	–	–	0.451* (0.235)	–	–	–	0.407 (0.259)	–
log (*InvDisc/ Research*)	–	–	0.437** (0.189)	–	–	–	0.420** (0.195)	–
log (*Basic*)	–	–	–	0.404* (0.237)	–	–	–	0.368 (0.251)
log (*InvDisc/ Basic*)	–	–	–	0.439** (0.187)	–	–	–	0.420** (0.193)
DeptDOD	1.978*** (0.148)	2.271*** (0.521)	1.864*** (0.182)	1.864*** (0.164)	1.972*** (0.155)	2.255*** (0.521)	1.872*** (0.185)	1.849*** (0.168)
DeptDOE	2.467*** (0.251)	1.729*** (0.121)	1.721*** (0.138)	1.736*** (0.129)	2.458*** (0.259)	1.738*** (0.119)	1.737*** (0.144)	1.746*** (0.131)
GR	–	–	–	–	−0.014 (0.090)	−0.036 (0.096)	−0.045 (0.106)	−0.049 (0.099)
Intercept	−6.061* (2.986)	3.821 (1.848)	1.637 (1.806)	2.027	−5.890* (3.364)	3.904 (2.991)	2.004 (2.055)	2.316 (1.920)
R^2	0.947	0.947	0.945	0.945	0.947	0.946	0.945	0.946

Note: *** significant at .01-level or better, ** significant at .05-level, * significant at .10-level. Regression results incorporate a first-order autoregressive correction.

With reference to the estimated regression coefficient in column (1), a 10 percent increase in the ratio of new invention disclosures to STEM employees (*InvDisc/Emp*) is associated with a 4.87 percent increase in patent applications (*PatApps*); a 10 percent increase in the ratio of new invention disclosures to total investments in R&D (*InvDisc/R&D*) is associated with a 4.34 percent increase in patent applications; a 10 percent increase in the ratio of new inven-

tion disclosures to investments in research (*InvDisc/Research*) is associated
with a 4.37 percent increase in patent applications; and a 10 percent increase in
the ratio of new invention disclosures to investments in basic research (*InvDisc/
Basic*) is associated with a 4.39 percent increase in patent applications.[12]

From the results reported in columns (5) through (8) of Table 5.11, which
are based on the same models as in columns (1) through (4) except that the
Great Recession variable (*GR*) is also held constant; *GR* equals 1 for FY2008,
FY2009, and FY2010 and 0 otherwise. The estimated coefficient on *GR* is
not significantly different from zero in any specification. These findings are
not inconsistent with the interpretation from Figure 5.5 that there is no visual
evidence of a Great Recession effect on new patent applications at DOD, DOE,
and NASA.

There are at least two ways to interpret the elasticity values from Table 5.11.
At one level, the findings reinforce the knowledge transfer effect of new invention disclosures on the technology transfer mechanism of patent applications.
The decision to patent reflects the scientists' and the laboratory's judgment
about the importance of the developed technology, whereas licensing and
research collaborations reflect also the market demand for the developed technology. At another level, the findings may be broadly interpreted as reflecting
an example of public sector entrepreneurial action.

Hébert and Link (2009), based on their historical overview of the scholarly
writings about who the entrepreneur is and what he/she does, offered a definition of an entrepreneur as one who perceives an opportunity *and* has the
ability to act on that perception. In other words, entrepreneurial action involves
both perception and action. I introduced in Chapter 3 the concept of public
sector entrepreneurship to refer to the perception and action of a public sector
individual whose action changed the status quo economic environment for the
social good. The general definition of an entrepreneur and the specific notion
of public sector entrepreneurship are similar. With reference to the findings in
Table 5.11, a scientist within a federal laboratory perceived a research opportunity as revealed through an invention disclosure, and the laboratory acted
on that perception through its patent application. The laboratory must have
envisioned social value of possibly patenting the scientist's invention idea or it
would not have incurred the cost of applying for a patent.

SUMMARY

This chapter presented a descriptive analysis of federal laboratory technology
transfer mechanisms and metrics for each of the 11 major federal agencies,
and an analytical analysis of that relationship for DOD, DOE, and NASA.
From a descriptive perspective, I do not think that one can generalize about
the relationship between the Great Recession and trends in technology transfer

activity from federal laboratories in general. However, from a statistical point of view, new empirical evidence was presented on the relationship between appropriately denominated new invention disclosures and patent applications.

As discussed in Chapter 1, not all federally funded technologies emanate from the research conducted in federal laboratories. Chapter 6 provides institutional background on federally funded research projects in small firms, funded through the Small Business Innovation Research (SBIR) program and Small Business Technology Transfer (STTR) program.

NOTES

1. The origin of the IAWGTT traces to President Reagan's April 10, 1987 Executive Order 12591, Facilitating Access to Science and Technology as discussed in Chapter 1. Recall that agencies are required to submit to the President and the Congress, through the Technology Partnerships Office at NIST, annual reports summarizing their technology transfer activities.
2. FY2020 is the last fiscal year of data available from the Technology Partnerships Office at NIST as of the time of writing this book. Data on FY2020 might not be comparable to data from previous fiscal years because it captures research activity associated with Covid-19.
3. See https://www.nist.gov/document/2020-technology-transfer-report-guidance, accessed December 2, 2022.
4. As written in the U.S. Code: "Each Federal agency may permit the director of any of its Government-operated Federal laboratories, and, to the extent provided in an agency-approved joint work statement or, if permitted by the agency, in an agency-approved annual strategic plan, the director of any of its Government-owned, contractor-operated laboratories—(1) to enter into cooperative research and development agreements on behalf of such agency (subject to subsection (c) of this section) with other Federal agencies; units of State or local government; industrial organizations (including corporations, partnerships, and limited partnerships, and industrial development organizations); public and private foundations; nonprofit organizations (including universities); or other persons (including licensees of inventions owned by the Federal agency) …"
5. See https://ncses.nsf.gov/pubs/ncses22209, accessed December 6, 2022.
6. For a policy discussion of invention disclosures affecting patent applications, see GAO (2018).
7. The correlation coefficient between *R&D* and *Emp* across DOD, DOE, and NASA is 0.289 (p =.039).
8. This production model is an adaptation of the production model used by Hall and Ziedonis (2001), Czarnitzki et al. (2009), and Link et al. (2019).
9. The right-hand side of equation (5.1) is multiplied by $(Emp^{\beta}/Emp^{\beta}) = 1$.
10. The right-hand side of equations (5.2) through (5.4) is multiplied by $(R\&D^{\beta}/R\&D^{\beta})$, $(Research^{\beta}/Research^{\beta})$, and $(Basic^{\beta}/Basic^{\beta})$, respectively. Each of these three ratios equals 1.
11. NASA fixed effects are subsumed in the intercept term.
12. The mean value of $(InvDisc/Emp) = 0.194$; the mean value of $(InvDisc/R\&D) = 0.083$; the mean value of $(InvDisc/Research) = 0.198$; and the mean value of $(InvDisc/Basic) = 0.456$.

6. Publicly funded small business research programs

LEGISLATIVE BACKGROUND

The Small Business Act of 1953 (Title II, Section 202 of Public Law 163) states:

> The essence of the American economic system of private enterprise is free competition. Only through full and free competition can free markets, free entry into business, and opportunities for the expression and growth of personal initiative and individual judgment be assured. The preservation and expansion of such competition is basic not only to the economic well-being but to the security of this Nation. Such security and well-being cannot be realized unless the actual and potential capacity of small business is encouraged and developed. It is the declared policy of the Congress that the Government should aid, counsel, assist, and protect insofar as is possible the interests of *small-business concerns* [emphasis added] in order to preserve free competitive enterprise, to insure [*sic*] that a fair proportion of the total purchases and contracts for supplies and services for the Government be placed with small-business enterprises, and to maintain and strengthen the overall economy of the Nation ... In order to carry out the policies of this title there is hereby created an agency under the name "Small Business Administration [SBA]."

The Small Business Act of 1958 withdrew Title II of Public Law 163, and it legislated a separate Act called the Small Business Act. After amendments to the Small Business Act, the legislation was amended again through Public Law 97–219, the Small Business Innovation Development Act of 1982.

The so-called Act of 1982 states the following about small businesses and the purpose of the Act:

> The Congress finds that—
> (1) technological innovation creates jobs, increases productivity, competition, and economic growth, and is a valuable counterforce to inflation and the United States balance-of-payments deficit;
> (2) while small business is the principal source of significant innovations in the Nation, the vast majority of federally funded research and development is

conducted by large businesses, universities, and Government laboratories; and

(3) small businesses are among the most cost-effective performers of research and development and are particularly capable of developing research and development results into new products.

Therefore, the purposes of the Act are—

(1) to stimulate technological innovation;
(2) to use small business to meet Federal research and development needs;
(3) to foster and encourage participation by minority and disadvantaged persons in technological innovation; and
(4) to increase private sector commercialization innovations derived from Federal research and development.

The Small Business Innovation Research (SBIR) program is explicitly defined in the Act of 1982, and the current version of the program has been discussed in detail in, for example, Leyden and Link (2015), Link and Scott (2012), and Link and Van Hasselt (2023).[1] As stated in the Act of 1982:

... the term "Small Business Innovation Research Program" or "SBIR" means a program under which a portion of a Federal agency's research or research and development effort is reserved for awards to small business concerns through a uniform process having—(A) a first phase for determining, insofar as possible, the scientific and technical merit and feasibility of ideas submitted pursuant to SBIR program solicitations; (B) a second phase to further develop the proposed ideas to meet the particular program needs, the awarding of which shall take into consideration the scientific and technical merit and feasibility evidenced by the first phase and, where two or more proposals are evaluated as being of approximately equal scientific and technical merit and feasibility, special consideration shall be given to those proposals that have demonstrated a third phase, non-Federal capital commitments; and (C) where appropriate, a third phase in which non-Federal capital pursues commercial applications of the research or research and development and which may also involve follow-on non-SBIR funded production contracts with a Federal agency for products or processes intended for use by the United States Government; and (5) the term "research" or "research and development" means any activity which is (A) a systematic, intensive study directed toward greater knowledge or understanding of the subject studied; (B) a systematic study directed specifically toward applying new knowledge to meet a recognized need; or (C) a systematic application of knowledge toward the production of useful materials, devices, and systems or methods, including design, development, and improvement of prototypes and new processes to meet specific requirements.

The Small Business Research and Development Enhancement Act of 1992 (Public Law 102–564) amended the Act of 1982. Title II of this Act is cited as the Small Business Technology Transfer Act of 1992, and it established the Small Business Technology Transfer Pilot Program:

> Term "Small Business Technology Transfer Program" or "STTR" means a pilot program under which a portion of a Federal agency's extramural research or research and development effort is reserved for award to small business concerns for cooperative research and development[2] through a uniform process having—(A) a first phase [Phase I], to determine, to the extent possible, the scientific, technical, and commercial merit and feasibility of ideas submitted pursuant to STTR program solicitations; (B) a second phase [Phase II], to further develop proposed ideas to meet particular program needs, in which awards shall be made based on the scientific, technical, and commercial merit and feasibility of the idea, as evidenced by the first phase and by other relevant information; and (C) where appropriate, a third phase—
>
> (i)   in which commercial applications of STTR funded research or research and development are funded by non-Federal sources of capital or, for products or services intended for use by the Federal Government, by follow-on non-STTR Federal funding awards; and
>
> (ii)   for which awards from non-STTR Federal funding sources are used for the continuation of research or research and development that has been competitively selected using peer review or scientific review criteria ...

The SBIR program and the STTR program have been reauthorized several times.[3] Most recently, the National Defense Authorization Act for Fiscal Year 2017 (Public Law 114–328) extended the SBIR and STTR programs until September 2022. On September 20, 2022, the Senate passed S. 4900 to extend the SBIR program and the STTR program through September 30, 2025, and the House of Representatives also passed that bill. The SBIR and STTR Extension Act of 2022 (Public Law 117–183) was signed by President Joseph Biden on September 30, 2022.[4]

The set-aside amount of extramural research funding for the STTR program is 0.45 percent compared to 3.2 percent for the SBIR program, but an agency may exceed this percentage. The current guideline amounts for Phase I and Phase II awards are $150,000 for Phase I projects and $1 million for Phase II projects. However, awards may not exceed guideline amounts by more than 50 percent ($225,000 for Phase I and $1.5 million for Phase II), and agencies must report all awards exceeding the guideline amounts and must receive a special waiver from the Small Business Administration (SBA) to exceed the guideline amounts by more than 50 percent.[5]

The Congressional Research Service (CRS, 2022) recently elaborated on Phase I and Phase II activities from what was included in the Act of 1992. Simply, Phase I awards support proof of concept research,[6] and Phase II awards extend the Phase I research with the goal of the funded project resulting in a commercializable technology.

For completeness and preciseness, the CRS (2022, pp. 4–5) defined Phase I and Phase II awards for the SBIR program as:

> In Phase I, an agency solicits contract proposals or grant applications to conduct feasibility-related experimental or theoretical research or research and development (R/R&D) related to agency requirements. The scope of the topic(s) in the solicitation may be broad or narrow, depending on the needs of the agency. Phase I grants are intended to determine "the scientific and technical merit and feasibility of ideas that appear to have commercial potential." Generally, SBIR Phase I awards are not to exceed $150,000, adjusted for inflation, though the law provides agencies with the authority to issue awards that exceed this amount (the Phase I award guideline) by as much as 50%. In addition, agencies may request a waiver from the SBA to exceed the award guideline by more than 50% for a specific topic.[7] In general, the period of performance for Phase I awards is up to six months, though agencies may allow for a longer performance period for a particular project.
>
> Phase II grants are intended to further R/R&D efforts initiated in Phase I that meet particular program needs and that exhibit potential for commercial application. In general, only Phase I grant recipients are eligible for Phase II grants. There are two exceptions to this guideline: (1) a federal agency may issue an SBIR Phase II award to a Small Business Technology Transfer (STTR) Phase I awardee to further develop the work performed under the STTR Phase I award; and (2) through FY2025, the National Institutes of Health (NIH), DOD, and ED are authorized to make Phase II grants to small businesses that did not receive Phase I awards. Exercise of either of these exceptions requires a determination from the agency head that the small business has demonstrated the scientific and technical merit and feasibility of the ideas and that the ideas appear to have commercial potential. Phase II awards are to be based on the results achieved in Phase I (when applicable) and the scientific and technical merit and commercial potential of the project proposed in Phase II as evidenced by: the small business concern's record of successfully commercializing SBIR or other research; the existence of second phase funding commitments from private sector or non-SBIR funding sources; the existence of third phase, follow-on commitments for the subject of the research; and the presence of other indicators of the commercial potential of the idea. The *Policy Directive* generally limits SBIR Phase II awards to $1 million, adjusted for inflation (the Phase II award guideline), though the directive provides agencies with the authority to issue an award that exceeds this amount by as much as 50%. As with Phase I grants, agencies may request a waiver from the SBA to exceed the Phase II award guideline by more than 50% for a specific topic.[8] In general, the period of performance for Phase II awards is not to exceed two years, though agencies may allow for a longer performance period for a particular project. Agencies may make a sequential Phase II award to continue the work of an initial Phase II award. The amount of a sequential Phase II award is subject to the same Phase II award guideline and agencies' authority to exceed the guideline by up to 50%. Thus, agencies may award up to $3 million, adjusted for inflation, in Phase II awards for a particular project to a single recipient at the agency's discretion, and potentially more if the agency requests and receives a waiver from the SBA. For sequential Phase II awards, some agencies require third party matching of the agency's SBIR funds.

And Phase I and Phase II awards for the STTR program as CRS (2022, pp. 14–15):

> In Phase I, an agency solicits contract proposals or grant applications to conduct feasibility-related experimental or theoretical research or research and development (R/R&D) related to agency requirements. The scope of the topic(s) in the solicitation may be broad or narrow, depending on the needs of the agency. Phase I grants are intended to determine "the scientific and technical merit and feasibility of the proposed effort and the quality of performance of the [small business] with a relatively small agency investment before consideration of further Federal support in Phase II." Generally, STTR Phase I awards are limited to the same award guideline amount as SBIR Phase I awards (see "SBIR Phases" above). Similar to SBIR Phase I awards, agencies may issue STTR Phase I awards that exceed the guideline amount by as much as 50% and may request a waiver from the SBA to exceed the award guideline by more than 50% for a specific topic.[9] In general, the period of performance for Phase I awards is not to exceed one year, though agencies may allow for a longer performance period for a particular project.
>
> Phase II grants are intended to further R/R&D efforts initiated in Phase I that meet particular program needs and that exhibit potential for commercial application. In general, only Phase I grant recipients are eligible for Phase II grants. Awards are to be based on the results achieved in Phase I and the scientific and technical merit and commercial potential of the project proposed in Phase II. The *Policy Directive* generally limits STTR Phase II awards to $1 million, adjusted for inflation (the Phase II award guideline). As with Phase I grants, agencies may issue awards that exceed this guideline by as much as 50% and may request a waiver from the SBA to exceed the guideline by more than 50% for a specific topic.[10] In general, the period of performance for Phase II awards is not to exceed two years, though agencies may allow for a longer performance period for a particular project. Agencies may make a sequential Phase II award to continue the work of an initial Phase II award. This sequential Phase II award is also subject to the Phase II award guideline amount and agencies' authority to exceed the guideline by up to 50%. Thus, agencies may award up to $3 million, adjusted for inflation, in Phase II awards for a particular project to a single recipient at the agency's discretion, and potentially more if the agency requests and receives a waiver from the SBA. For sequential Phase II awards, some agencies require third-party matching of the agency's STTR funds.

There is a Phase III for both the SBIR and STTR programs. Again, for completeness and preciseness, Phase III for the SBIR program is described as (CRS, 2022, p. 5):

> Phase III of the SBIR program is focused on the commercialization of results achieved with Phase I and Phase II SBIR funding. The SBIR program does not provide funding in Phase III. Phase III funding is expected, generally, to be generated in the private sector. However, some agencies may use non-SBIR funds for Phase III funding to support additional R&D or contracts for products, processes, or services intended for use by the federal government. In addition, the law directs agencies and prime contractors "to the greatest extent practicable," to facilitate the

commercialization of SBIR and STTR projects through the use of Phase III awards, including sole source awards.

And for the STTR program, Phase III is described as (CRS, 2022, p. 15):

> Phase III of the STTR program is focused on the commercialization of the results achieved through Phase I and Phase II STTR funding. The STTR program does not provide funding in Phase III. Phase III funding is expected, generally, to be generated in the private sector. However, some agencies may use non-STTR funds for Phase III funding to support additional R&D or contracts for products, processes, or services intended for use by the federal government. In addition, the law directs agencies and prime contractors "to the greatest extent practicable," to facilitate the commercialization of SBIR and STTR projects through the use of Phase III awards, including sole source awards.

As described by the SBA,[11] the purposes of the STTR program are similar to the purposes of the SBIR program as stated above with the exception that purpose statement (3) has been modified to "[f]oster and encourage participation in innovation and entrepreneurship by women and socially or economically disadvantaged persons."[12] In addition, the purpose of the STTR program is to:[13]

> ... facilitate the transfer of technology developed by a research institution through the entrepreneurship of a small business concern (SBC).

More specifically:[14]

> Central to the STTR program is the partnership between small businesses and nonprofit research institutions. The STTR program requires the small business to formally collaborate with a research institution in Phase I and Phase II [as defined above]. STTR's most important role is to bridge the gap between performance of basic science and commercialization of resulting innovations.

Regarding eligibility to apply for an SBIR award or an STTR award, a firm must have fewer than 500 employees, including employees of affiliates. In addition, the firm must be (CRS, 2021, p. 15):

(1)   more than 50% directly owned and controlled by one or more citizens or permanent resident aliens of the United States, other small business concerns (each of which is more than 50% directly owned and controlled by individuals who are citizens or permanent resident aliens of the United States), an Indian tribe, Alaskan Native Corporation (ANC), or Native Hawaiian Organization (NHO), a wholly owned business entity of such tribe, ANC, or NHO, or any combination of these; or

(2)   a joint venture in which each entity to the joint venture meets the requirements in paragraph (1) above.

The transfer of the technical knowledge developed through the basic sciences in Phase I and the transfer of the technology itself developed in Phase II occurs through the commercialization of the resulting technology as an innovation. Thus, one might think of technology as the application of new knowledge, learned through the basic sciences, to some practical problem, and innovation as technology put into use or commercialized.

Link and Scott (2012) have previously offered a theoretical market failure framework for understanding the economics of the SBIR program. However, their arguments apply equally well to the STTR program and are summarized below.

Market failure—a defining concept for this book—with respect to investing in R&D, is manifested in terms of firms underinvesting in R&D from society's perspective. The underinvestment occurs because conditions exist that prevent the investing firm from fully realizing or appropriating the benefits or returns created by their investments. Arrow (1962, p. 609) identified three sources of market failure related to knowledge-based innovative activity: "indivisibilities, inappropriability, and uncertainty." In more detail, consider a marketable technology to be produced in a firm through an R&D process where there are conditions that prevent the firm from fully appropriating the returns from the marketed technology. Because of a lack of appropriability, other firms in the market or in a related market will realize some of the returns (i.e., profits) from the firm's research and its innovation(s). The R&D-investing firm will realize that, because of conditions that prevent it from fully appropriating the return to its investments, the marginal benefits it can receive from investing in such R&D will be less than it could earn in the absence of such conditions. As a result, the firm might underinvest, from a social perspective, in R&D. The STTR program, through its Phase I and Phase II awards, is in a sense subsidizing the firm (i.e., lowering the marginal cost of research) to incentivize it to undertake the socially desirable level of R&D investments.

SBIR AND STTR PROGRAM METRICS

Table 6.1 shows the number of Phase I and Phase II awards for both the SBIR and STTR programs in FY2021. Clearly, the SBIR program is larger not only in terms of number of awards but also in terms of award and obligated amounts. The age and size of the SBIR program are likely the reasons that the program receives more visibility in the policy and small business environment than does the STTR program.

Table 6.1   *Metrics on the SBIR program and STTR program for fiscal*
                   year 2021

Metric	SBIR Program	STTR Program
Awards		
	$3,438	$988
	$2,057	$300
Total award and obligated amount ($M)		
	$643.3	$189.8
	$722.3	$333.3

Source: https://www.sbir.gov, accessed January 25, 2023.

The first Phase I SBIR award was in 1983, and the first Phase II award was in 1984. The first Phase I STTR award was in 1995 (one award in 1995 and one award in 1996), and the first Phase II award was in 1986. Figures 6.1 through 6.4 show the number of awards by fiscal year. The number of Phase I SBIR and STTR awards shown in Figures 6.1 and 6.2 have been increasing over time. However, the number of Phase I awards began to decrease prior to the Great Recession. In recent years only the number of Phase I STTR awards has been above trend.

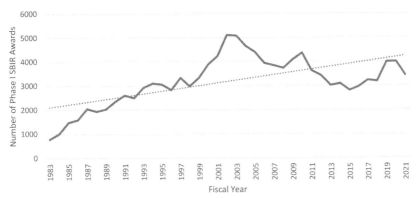

Note: The dotted line is an Excel-generated trend line.
Source: https://www.sbir.gov, accessed January 26, 2023.

Figure 6.1   *Number of Phase I SBIR awards, by fiscal year*
                   FY1983–FY2021

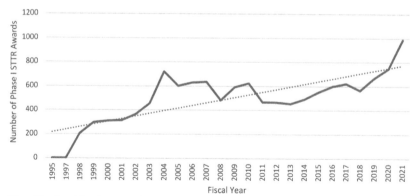

Note: The dotted line is an Excel-generated trend line.
Source: https://www.sbir.gov, accessed January 26, 2023.

Figure 6.2   *Number of Phase I STTR awards, by fiscal year
                  FY1995–FY2021*

Figures 6.3 and 6.4 both show a decline in Phase II awards during the Great
Recession, but those SBIR and STTR declines were exacerbated by the decline
in Phase I awards prior to the Great Recession.

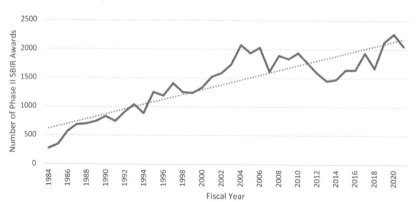

Note: The dotted line is an Excel-generated trend line.
Source: https://www.sbir.gov, accessed January 26, 2023.

Figure 6.3   *Number of Phase II SBIR awards, by fiscal year
                  FY1984–FY2021*

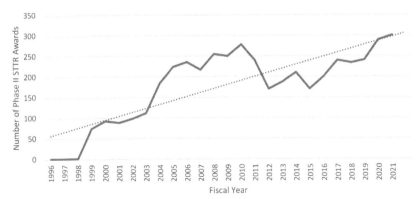

Note: The dotted line is an Excel-generated trend line.
Source: https://www.sbir.gov, accessed January 26, 2023.

Figure 6.4   *Number of Phase II STTR awards, by fiscal year FY1996–FY2021*

Similar Phase I and Phase II SBIR and STTR trends in award and obligation amounts are shown in Figures 6.5 through 6.8 (keeping in mind that the award and obligation amounts are in current dollars rather than real inflation-adjusted dollars). The trend in award and obligation amounts parallels the trend in the number of awards.

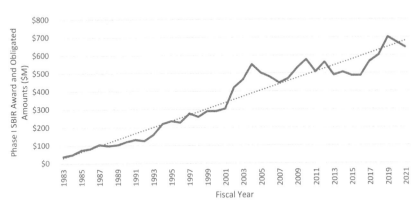

Note: The dotted line is an Excel-generated trend line.
Source: https://www.sbir.gov, accessed January 26, 2023.

Figure 6.5   *Total Phase I SBIR award and obligated amounts ($ millions), by fiscal year FY1983–FY2021*

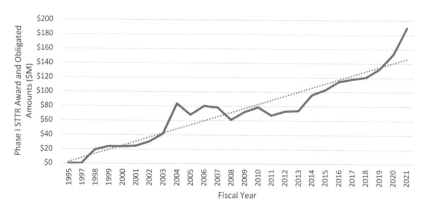

Note: The dotted line is an Excel-generated trend line.
Source: https://www.sbir.gov, accessed January 26, 2023.

Figure 6.6   *Total Phase I STTR award and obligated amounts
                    ($ millions), by fiscal year FY1995–FY2021*

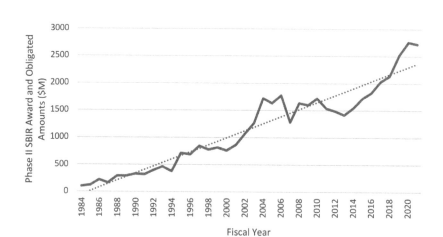

Note: The dotted line is an Excel-generated trend line.
Source: https://www.sbir.gov, accessed January 26, 2023.

Figure 6.7   *Total Phase II SBIR award and obligated amounts
                    ($ millions), by fiscal year FY1984–FY2021*

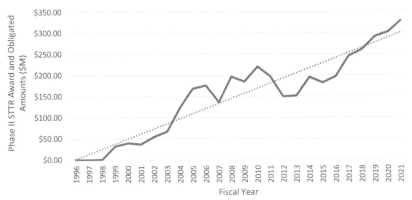

Note: The dotted line is an Excel-generated trend line.
Source: https://www.sbir.gov, accessed January 26, 2023.

Figure 6.8   *Total Phase II STTR award and obligated amounts
($ millions), by fiscal year FY1996–FY2021*

THE NRC DATABASES

Much of the empirical academic and policy literature that is related to the SBIR and STTR programs has relied on data collected by the National Research Council (NRC) within the U.S. National Academies of Sciences, Engineering, and Medicine (generally referred to as the National Academies).[15,16] As background, the NRC was charged in 2000 with the collection of SBIR program-specific data. The NRC wrote in its report to Congress (National Research Council, 2008, p. 13):

> As the Small Business Innovation Research (SBIR) program approached its twentieth year of operation, the U.S. Congress asked the National Research Council (NRC) to carry out a "comprehensive study of how the SBIR program has stimulated technological innovation and used small businesses to meet federal research and development needs" and make recommendations on improvements to the program.

More formally, authority for this NRC study, which has become known as the first-round assessment of the SBIR program, was a part of the Small Business

Innovation Research Program Reauthorization Act of 2000 (Public Law 106–554):

> Congress finds that—
> (1)   the small business innovation research program established under the Small Business Innovation Development Act of 1982, and reauthorized by the Small Business Research and Development Enhancement Act of 1992 … is highly successful in involving small businesses in federally funded research and development;
> (2)   the SBIR program made the cost-effective and unique research and development capabilities possessed by the small businesses of the Nation available to Federal agencies and departments;
> (3)   the innovative goods and services developed by small businesses that participated in the SBIR program have produced innovations of critical importance in a wide variety of high-technology fields, including biology, medicine, education, and defense;
> (4)   the SBIR program is a catalyst in the promotion of research and development, the commercialization of innovative technology, the development of new products and services, and the continued excellence of this Nation's high-technology industries; and
> (5)   the continuation of the SBIR program will provide expanded opportunities for one of the Nation's vital resources, its small businesses, will foster invention, research, and technology, will create jobs, and will increase this Nation's competitiveness in international markets.
> The Administration is to collect such information from awardees as is necessary to assess the SBIR program …

Among other activities in response to its Congressional charge, the NRC collected information from a random sample of Phase II awardees funded by Department of Defense (DOD), National Institutes of Health (NIH), National Aeronautics and Space Administration (NASA), Department of Energy (DOE), and National Science Foundation (NSF) over the fiscal year time period 1992 thought 2001 on a number of aspects of the awardees and on dimensions of their funded Phase II research projects. The collected information was codified into what is called the 2005 Database, and it was made available for study by selected researchers.[17]

In Section 5137, Continued Evaluation by the National Academy of Sciences, of the National Defense Authorization Act for Fiscal Year 2012 (Public Law 112–81), Congress again charged the NRC to study the SBIR and STTR programs (National Academies of Sciences, Engineering, and Medicine, 2016, p. 21):

> … to review the Small Business Innovation Research and Small Business Technology Transfer (SBIR/STTR) programs at the Department of Defense, the National Institutes of Health, the National Aeronautics and Space Administration, the Department of Energy, and the National Science Foundation. Building on the

outcomes from the first-round study, this second-round [assessment] study is to examine both topics of general policy interest that emerged during the first-round study and topics of specific interest to individual agencies.

As was done for the first-round study, the NRC again collected information from Phase II awardees on a number of aspects of the awardees and on their funded research projects. In 2011, as the first part of the second-round study of the SBIR program, Phase II projects funded by DOD, NASA, and NSF were surveyed; in 2014, Phase II projects funded by NIH and DOE were surveyed. The survey information from these agency studies was codified into what is referred to, respectively, the 2011 Database and the 2014 Database.

For the construction of both the 2005 Database, the 2011 Database, and the 2014 Database, the NRC implemented a process to select a random sample of Phase II awards from the five agencies with the largest SBIR programs: DOD, NIH, NASA, DOE, and NSF.[18]

The years covered for each agency differ based on the timing of the 2011 and 2014 surveys. For DOD, the years covered are 1992–2007, for NIH the years covered are 1992–2010, for NASA the years covered are 1992–2007, for DOE the years covered are 1992–2010, and for NSF the years covered are 1992–2009. Table 6.2 shows the number of SBIR and STTR Phase II projects included in the Databases, by agency.

Table 6.2   *Phase II projects included in the NRC Databases*

	DOD	NIH	NASA	DOE	NSF
Phase II SBIR projects	1,685	401	360	1,068	571
Phase II STTR projects	107	36	18	112	23
Total	1,792	437	378	1,180	594

Note: Data, relevant for the analysis in the following chapters, were not reported to the NRC by the firms associated with some projects.
Source: NRC Databases discussed above

SUMMARY

Not all federally funded technologies emanate from the research conducted in federal laboratories or even funded by the laboratory's host agencies. In this chapter, institution and legislative background was presented on the Small Business Innovation Research (SBIR) program and the Small Business Technology Transfer (STTR) program.

Chapter 7 relies on NRC data on SBIR and STTR research projects to describe the knowledge transfers and technology transfer from publicly funded and privately performed research projects.

NOTES

1. The description of the Small Business Innovation Research (SBIR) program builds on the description in Link and Van Hasselt (2023).
2. The Act of 1992 defines the term *cooperative research and development* as: "research or research and development conducted jointly by a small business concern and a research institution in which not less than 40 percent of the work is performed by the small business concern, and not less than 30 percent of the work is performed by the research institution"; and the term *research institution* refers to "a nonprofit institution, as defined in section 4(5) of the Stevenson-Wydler Technology Innovation Act of 1980, and includes federally funded research and development centers, as identified by the National Scientific Foundation in accordance with the governmentwide Federal Acquisition Regulation issued in accordance with section 35(c)(1) of the Office of Federal Procurement Policy Act." The research institution must also be located in the United States (CRS, 2021).
3. See Link and Van Hasselt (2023) for a detailed history of the reauthorization of the SBIR program.
4. The Act "… requires agencies with an SBIR or STTR program to establish a due diligence program to assess the potential risk posed by program applicants' foreign ties; requires certain departments and agencies to report on national security risks within their SBIR/STTR programs; and establishes increased minimum performance standards for firms that have won a certain number of awards during a specified period of time." More specifically, the new legislation points to firms that have had multiple Phase II awards (so-called *mills*): "Not later than 18 months after the date of enactment of this Act, the Comptroller General of the United States shall conduct a study and submit to the Committee on Small Business and Entrepreneurship of the Senate and the Committee on Small Business and the Committee on Science, Space, and Technology of the House of Representatives a report, which shall be made publicly available, on small business concerns that are awarded not less than 50 Phase II awards under the SBIR or STTR programs during the consecutive period of 10 fiscal years preceding the most recent 2 fiscal years …"
5. See https://www.sba.gov/content/key-changes-sbir-and-sttr-policy-directives, accessed January 25, 2023.
6. My thanks to John Jankowski, former Director of the R&D Statistics Program at NSF, for sharing with me his professional view that proof of concept research probably "falls in the end of the applied research spectrum." For reference, the OECD's Frascati Manual does not define proof of concept research. See https://www.oecd.org/innovation/frascati-manual-2015-9789264239012-en.htm, accessed February 25, 2023.
7. As of November 2021, an agency may issue a Phase I award up to $275,766 without seeking a waiver from the Small Business Administration (SBA).
8. As of November 2021, an agency may issue a Phase II award up to $1,838,436 without seeking a waiver from the SBA.

9.   As of November 2021, an agency may issue a Phase I award up to $275,766 without seeking a waiver from the SBA.

10.   As of November 2021, an agency may issue a Phase II award up to $1,838,436 without seeking a waiver from the SBA.

11.   See https://www.sbir.gov/tutorials/program-basics/tutorial-1, accessed January 25, 2023.

12.   See https://seedfund.nsf.gov/fastlane/definitions/, accessed January 25, 2023. "A member of any of the following groups: Black Americans, Hispanic Americans, Native Americans, Asian-Pacific Americans, Subcontinent Asian Americans, other groups designated from time to time by the Small Business Administration (SBA) to be socially disadvantaged, and any other individual found to be socially and economically disadvantaged by SBA pursuant to Section 8(a) of the Small Business Act, 15 U.S.C.; 637(a)."

13.   The applicant for an STTR award is always a small business. The STTR program requires that the small business and its partnering institution establish an intellectual property agreement detailing the intellectual property rights and the right to continue with follow-on research, development, or commercialization activity. See https://www.sbir.gov/faqs/general-questions, accessed January 25, 2023.

14.   See https://www.sbir.gov/about#sbir-policy-directive, accessed January 25, 2023.

15.   This section of the chapter draws directly from Link (2023b) and Link and Van Hasselt (2023).

16.   "The National Research Council was organized by the National Academy of Sciences in 1916 to associate the broad community of science and technology with the Academy's purposes of further knowledge and advising the federal government. The Council has become the principal operating agency of both the National Academy of Sciences and the National Academy of Engineering in providing services to the government, the public, and the scientific and engineering communities." See https://history.aip.org/phn/21511003.html, accessed January 28, 2023.

17.   A table of the extant literature using Phase II project information in the 2005 Database is in Link and Van Hasselt (2023).

18.   Care should be exercised when interpreting the survey responses based on how the adjective random is used by the National Academies to describe each database. A number of filters were imposed on the population of Phase II projects including the availability of known addresses of potential respondents. Thus, any generalizations from the descriptive statistics in the following chapters to all Phase II projects should be made with caution.

7. Knowledge transfers from publicly funded firms

INTRODUCTION

In the National Institute of Standards and Technology's (NIST) annual technology transfer report to the President and the Congress, there is an explicit mention of the economic benefits (i.e., to facilitate commercialization) associated with federal technology transfers (NIST, 2022, p. 1):

> Federal legislation provides a variety of *vehicles* [emphasis added] through which Federal technology transfer occurs. These vehicles facilitate the potential commercialization of inventions, enable the use of Federal laboratory facilities by non-Federal entities, and allow for the establishment of research partnerships between Federal laboratories and other entities.

Also stated in its annal report (NIST, 2022, p. 12), as previously noted, is that "most Federal research results are transferred through publication of S&E articles."

In this chapter, it is argued that two traditionally viewed technology transfer vehicles of patents received and scientific publications (i.e., publications in print) are more appropriately classified as knowledge transfer mechanisms rather than as vehicles for technology transfer.

As I pointed out in Chapter 2, the European Commission (2020, p. 8) characterized a knowledge transfer (KT) in the following way:

> KT is about getting research and expertise put to use which, by its nature is wide-ranging and complex.

The European Commission listed as examples of knowledge transfer indicators both publications and licenses, where licenses are, in my mind, the mechanism for transferring patented knowledge into the economy, and having it put into use.

Influencing my distinction between a knowledge transfer and a technology transfer traces to an argument that is nearly 40 years old. I wrote then that the concept of technology has indeed been used in a relatively narrow sense to describe physical tools of a certain sort, but it has also been used to describe a wide spectrum of social processes. Eschewing conceptualizations of technology that embrace social or other intangible entities allows one to think about the *knowledge* or information embodied in a technology (Bozeman and Link, 1983, p. 3):

> Any viable technological device may be viewed as a proof (of sorts) of the information assumptions that lead to its creation. The information embodied in a technology is diverse in regard to type, source, and instrumental application. … [S]ome of the information … is typically derived from well corroborated scientific theory [made public through scientific publications] but knowledge generated by scientists in pursuit of theory is rarely, if ever, sufficient for the more particular needs entailed in the construction of a technological device. Other sources of knowledge include information from controlled experimentation … from trial and error coupled with incremental and sometimes minute modifications … and information of the kind that goes under the rubrics of creativity, genius, and inspiration [as documented in patents].

As background, the following descriptions are offered:

* *Science*—the search for knowledge; the search is based on observed facts and truths; science begins with known starting conditions and searches for unknown end results.
* *Technology*—the application of knowledge, learned through science, to some practical problem.
* *Innovation*—technology put into use or commercialized as a product or process.

PATENTS RECEIVED AND SCIENTIFIC PUBLICATIONS OVER TIME

The data used to describe trends in patents received and scientific publications related to a Phase II project come from the National Research Council (NRC) Databases described in Chapter 6. The relevant survey questions are: *Please give the number of patents received and the number of scientific publications in print for the technology developed as a result of this Phase II project.*

Figures 7.1 through 7.5 illustrate patents received per Phase II project over the years of available data for each of the five agencies in the NRC Databases. The horizontal axis in these figures, and in those discussed below denotes the fiscal year of the Phase II award and not the fiscal year that a patent was awarded or that a publication came in print. The time dimension of the data in the NRC Databases prohibits a meaningful analysis of post-Great Recession analysis.

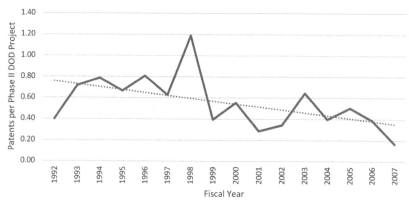

Note: The dotted line is an Excel-generated trend line.
Source: NRC Databases.

*Figure 7.1   Patents received per Phase II DOD project, by fiscal year
            FY1992–FY2007*

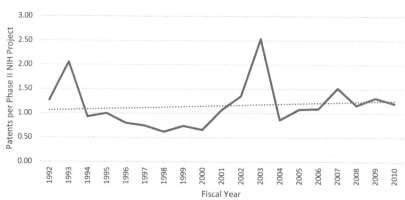

Note: The dotted line is an Excel-generated trend line.
Source: NRC Databases.

*Figure 7.2   Patents received per Phase II NIH project, by fiscal year
            FY1992–FY2010*

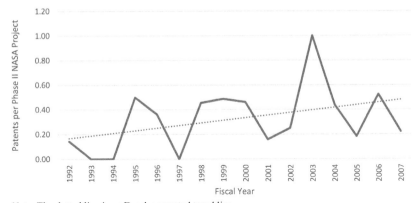

Note: The dotted line is an Excel-generated trend line.
Source: NRC Databases.

Figure 7.3   *Patents received per Phase II NASA project, by fiscal year*
                    FY1992–FY2007

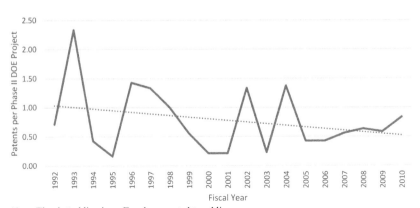

Note: The dotted line is an Excel-generated trend line.
Source: NRC Databases.

Figure 7.4   *Patents received per Phase II DOE project, by fiscal year*
                    FY1992–FY2010

One might be hard pressed to conclude from a visual inspection of the patents received per Phase II project data that the trend has been increasing over time. The one exception might be with regard to NASA funded projects.

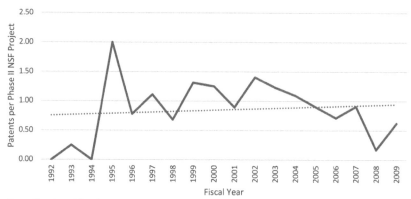

Note: The dotted line is an Excel-generated trend line.
Source: NRC Databases.

Figure 7.5   Patents received per Phase II NSF project, by fiscal year
FY1992–FY2009

Figures 7.6 through 7.10 illustrate publications per Phase II project over the years of available data for each agency. As with patents per Phase II project, publications per Phase II project have also not been increasing over time.

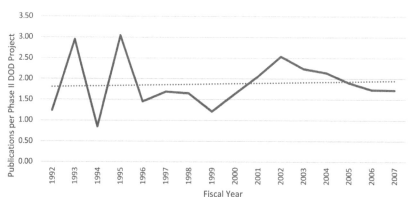

Note: The dotted line is an Excel-generated trend line.
Source: NRC Databases.

Figure 7.6   Publications per Phase II DOD project, by fiscal year
FY1992–FY2007

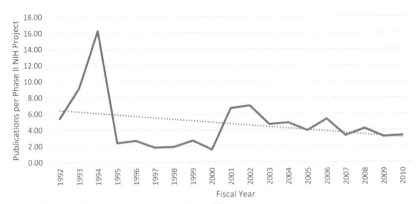

Note: The dotted line is an Excel-generated trend line.
Source: NRC Databases.

Figure 7.7   *Publications per Phase II NIH project, by fiscal year*
                  FY1992–FY2010

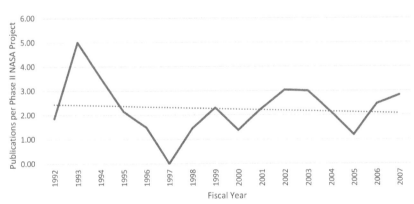

Note: The dotted line is an Excel-generated trend line.
Source: NRC Databases.

Figure 7.8   *Publications per Phase II NASA project, by fiscal year*
                  FY1992–FY2007

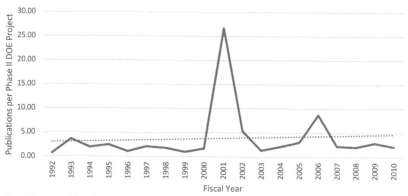

Note: The dotted line is an Excel-generated trend line.
Source: NRC Databases.

Figure 7.9   *Publications per Phase II DOE project, by fiscal year*
                  FY1992–FY2010

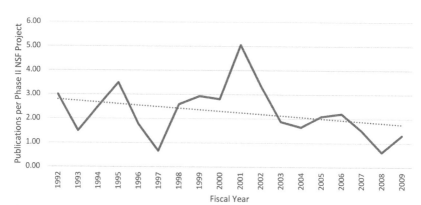

Note: The dotted line is an Excel-generated trend line.
Source: NRC Databases.

Figure 7.10   *Publications per Phase II NSF project, by fiscal year*
                  FY1992–FY2009

COVARIATES WITH PATENTING AND SCIENTIFIC PUBLISHING

In this section, firm and project characteristics associated with Phase II-related projects are correlated with patenting and publishing. From the NRC Databases two independent variables were constructed. The first variable measures whether or not there was *any* knowledge transfer from the Phase II project. This variable, *PatentorPublish*, equals 1 if the firm transferred knowledge from its Phase II project measured as there being at least one patent award *or* at least one scientific publication; and it equals 0 otherwise. The second variable measures if the firm patented *and* published from its Phase II project. This variable, *PatentandPublish*, equals 1 if the firm not only transferred knowledge through at least one patent award but also through at least one scientific publication; and it equals 0 otherwise.

Table 7.1 lists the variables used to estimate the relevant regression models,[1] and Table 7.2 shows descriptive statistics on the variables. The number of observations used in these models is less than the sampling population of Small Business Innovation (SBIR) and Small Business Technology Transfer (STTR) Phase II projects shown in Table 6.2. The reasons for the reduction in Phase II projects considered in the analysis below is (1) not all funded Phase II projects were completed; some of the projects failed; and (2) some of the key variables have missing values. A failed project is defined by an affirmative response to the survey statement:[2] *Efforts at this company have been discontinued. Not sales or additional funding results from this project.*

Table 7.1   Definition of key variables

Variable	Definition
PatentorPublish	= 1 if the Phase II project resulted in at least one patent or at least one publication related to the technology developed as a result of the Phase II project; 0 otherwise
PatentandPublish	= 1 if the Phase II project resulted in at least one patent and at least one publication related to the technology developed as a result of the Phase II project; 0 otherwise
Employment	Number of employees when the Phase II project was proposed
ProjectAge	Age of the Phase II project defined as the date of the NRC survey less the award date of the Phase II project
University	= 1 if a university or college was involved in the Phase II project in any way; 0 otherwise
DOD	= 1 if the Phase II project was funded through DOD; 0 otherwise
NIH	= 1 if the Phase II project was funded through NIH; 0 otherwise
NASA	= 1 if the Phase II project was funded through NASA; 0 otherwise
DOE	= 1 if the Phase II project was funded through DOE; 0 otherwise
NSF	= 1 if the Phase II project was funded through NSF; 0 otherwise

Note: DOD refers to the U.S. Department of Defense, NIH refers to the U.S. National Institutes of Health, NASA refers to the U.S. National Aeronautics and Space Administration, DOE refers to the U.S. Department of Energy, NSF refers to the U.S. National Science Foundation.

Table 7.2   Descriptive statistics on key variables (n = 2,923)

Variable	Mean	Standard Deviation	Minimum	Maximum
PatentorPublish	0.663	0.473	0	1
PatentandPublish	0.220	0.414	0	1
Employment	27.835	50.277	1	490
ProjectAge	6.962	2.643	2	13
University	0.425	0.494	0	1
DOD	0.411	0.492	0	1
NIH	0.247	0.431	0	1
NASA	0.087	0.281	0	1
DOE	0.092	0.290	0	1
NSF	0.164	0.370	0	1

Note: DOD refers to the U.S. Department of Defense, NIH refers to the U.S. National Institutes of Health, NASA refers to the U.S. National Aeronautics and Space Administration, DOE refers to the U.S. Department of Energy, NSF refers to the U.S. National Science Foundation.

Table 7.3 shows the Probit results that explain across-Phase II project difference in knowledge transfer activity as measured by the dependent variable *PatentorPublish*. NSF funded Phase II projects are subsumed in the intercept term. The independent variables *Employment* and *ProjectAge* entered the equation as natural logarithms to account for any nonlinearity.

Table 7.3   Probit regression results, dependent variable is PatentorPublish (n = 2,923) (p-values in parentheses, marginal effects in brackets)

Variable	Probit Results
ln(Employment)	−0.039
	(p = .033)
	[−0.014]
ln(ProjectAge)	0.241
	(p = .0002)
	[0.085]
University	0.371
	(p <.0001)
Intercept	−0.038
	(p = .782)
Agency effects	yes
Wald χ^2	110.89
	(p < .0001)

Focusing on the algebraic sign of the calculated marginal effects, the results suggest that smaller-sized firms, measured in terms of number of employees (a measure of human capital and firm size), are more likely to engage in knowledge transfers as measured by *PatentorPublish*. To the best of my knowledge, there is not a theoretical reason for this finding, but perhaps future scholars will focus on this smaller-firm behavior. Older projects, measured in terms of the number of years since the Phase II project was awarded, are more likely to engage in knowledge transfers as measured by *PatentorPublish*. It is likely that this finding reflects the fact that the researching firm had relatively more time to engage in successful patenting and publishing. Finally, Phase II projects that included the dichotomously measured use of university resources—and those resources included access to university-based human capital and technical capital that might not have been available within the researching firm—are more likely to engage in knowledge transfer as measured herein. The positive marginal effect on *University* perhaps reflects an internal resource enhancing impact from the use of university resources.

Table 7.4 show the Probit results that explain across-Phase II project difference in knowledge transfer activity as measured by the dependent variable *PatentandPublish*. As in Table 7.3, NSF funded Phase II projects are subsumed in the intercept term, and the independent variables *Employment* and *ProjectAge* entered the equation as natural logarithms to account for any nonlinearity.

Table 7.4   Probit regression results, dependent variable is PatentandPublish (n = 2,923) (p-values in parentheses, marginal effects in brackets)

Variable	Probit Results
ln(Employment)	−0.056
	(p = .006)
	[−0.016]
ln(ProjectAge)	0.294
	(p < .0001)
	[0.083]
University	0.247
	(p < .0001)
	[0.070]
Intercept	−1.120
	(p < .0001)
Agency effects	yes
Wald χ^2	126.87
	(p < .0001)

Before discussing the findings in Table 7.4, it might be important to justify why a firm, a small firm in particular, would both patent and publish findings about the technology developed during its Phase II project. One might argue that patenting is an important defense strategy for a small firm, but also one might be perplexed about publishing such defensive-intended information.

Hayter and Link (2022) have argued that a firm will use a patent as a formal and relatively effective (because of legal infringement protections and high visibility) intellectual property protection mechanism (IPPM) for its developed technology.[3] Simply put, patenting is a profit maximizing strategy.[4] Hayter and Link also acknowledged that the issue of publishing is more subtle, but it is still profit based. Publishing is an accretive and relatively less effective IPPM (because of no legal infringement protections and less visibility) when used by small firms (Hayter and Link, 2022, pp. 1368–9):

> Firms also employ so-called defensive publishing as a cost-effective strategy to invalidate would be patents among competitors, preserve their technological field of use, and provide competitive parity if they lag behind technologically … Defensive publishing is especially appealing to small firms given that they rarely have the resources to develop and sustain large patent portfolios.

The pattern of finding in Table 7.4 is similar to that in Table 7.3. The calculated marginal effect on *ln(Employment)* is negative, and it is positive on *ln(ProjectAge)* and *University*. One might view a small firm adopting a defensive strategy of both patenting and publishing as creative, and if so, then perhaps the economics and management literature referenced in Chapter 2 pertaining to creative responses emanating from the Great Recession may merit future study.

SUMMARY

The analysis in Chapter 7 identified correlations and covariates associated with knowledge transfers from small firms funded through the SBIR and STTR programs. Econometrics aside, the important finding from the analysis in this chapter is that public sector knowledge transfers and technology transfers should not exclusively be thought of in terms of the R&D-based activities of federal laboratories. Federally funded and privately performed R&D is also a candidate to illustrate the presence of spillover benefits from public dollars.

Chapter 8 introduces a previously unexplored dimension of federally funded technology that is transferred to other firms. This mechanism is the sale of rights to technology developed by SBIR and STTR funded research to other U.S. firms.

NOTES

1. A separate variable to distinguish between SBIR and STTR program projects was not included because all of the STTR funded projects in the NRC Databases included a university.
2. For a detailed study of Phase II project failures, see Link et al. (2022).
3. See Link and Van Hasselt (2020, 2022). See also Amoroso and Link (2021).
4. As Hayter and Link (2022, p. 1368) point out: "Firms [use] patents to signal dominant market strength and technical capability thus, preempting inventive activity and segmenting entry among competitors."

8. Technology transfers from publicly funded firms

INTRODUCTION

Information is available from the National Research Council (NRC) Databases about technology transfers in addition to the knowledge transfers discussed in Chapter 7. Specifically, the relevant survey question that I focus on in this chapter relates to whether the firm has a finalized agreement for the sale of the rights to the Phase II-developed technology, or whether the firm is engaged in ongoing negotiations for the sale of those rights.

This dimension of technology transfer has not previously been discussed in the Small Business Innovation Research (SBIR) or Small Business Technology Transfer (STTR) literature or in the broader technology transfer literature. Because of the newness of this metric and because the incidence of this behavior is limited (or rare, as discussed below), I treat either a final agreement or an ongoing negotiation as evidence of a technology transfer.

Only the data from the NRC 2005 Database are used in the analysis that follows. The NRC did not report the amount of each Phase II award in the 2011 Database or in the 2014 Database for confidential matters. The choice to use the 2005 Database allows for an exploration into the effect of the size of the Phase II award on the likelihood that the firm would engage in the form of technology transfer considered here, namely, the sale of the rights to the Phase II-developed technology. However, a downside of using the 2005 Database is that the most recent projects in the database were awarded in 2001; thus, the impact of the Great Recession on the likelihood of the sale of technology rights could not be considered.

EMPIRICAL ANALYSIS

The empirical analysis in this chapter explores covariates with the likelihood that a firm will transfer its Phase II-developed technology to another U.S. firm or U.S. investor. Table 8.1 defines this variable as well as other variables that are explored as possible covariates with this likelihood.

Table 8.1   Definition of key variables

Variable	Definition
USTechnologySales	= 1 if the Phase II project resulted in the final or ongoing sale of the developed technology to a U.S. firm/investor; 0 otherwise
Employment	Number of employees when the Phase II project was proposed
Award	Amount of the Phase II award in $2001 adjusted to real terms by the GDP deflator
PrevPhII	Number of previous Phase II awards related to the project/technology supported by the current Phase II project
PreviousPhII	= 1 if the firm had received at least one previous Phase II award related to the project/technology supported by the current Phase II project; 0 otherwise
PhaseIII	= 1 if the firm received additional developmental funding for the technology developed during the project; 0 otherwise
DOD	= 1 if the Phase II project was funded through DOD; 0 otherwise
NIH	= 1 if the Phase II project was funded through NIH; 0 otherwise
NASA	= 1 if the Phase II project was funded through NASA; 0 otherwise
DOE	= 1 if the Phase II project was funded through DOE; 0 otherwise
NSF	= 1 if the Phase II project was funded through NSF; 0 otherwise

Note: DOD refers to the U.S. Department of Defense, NIH refers to the U.S. National Institutes of Health, NASA refers to the U.S. National Aeronautics and Space Administration, DOE refers to the U.S. Department of Energy, NSF refers to the U.S. National Science Foundation.

As noted above, the operational definition of the sale of technology rights includes both finalized agreements as well as ongoing negotiations. The reason for this is that the incidence of either is rare. The mean value of finalized agreements is 0.034 (3.4 percent) and the mean value of ongoing negotiations is 0.071 (7.1 percent). Thus, as shown in Table 8.2, only 10.4 percent of the projects results in the sale of so-defined technology rights.[1]

Table 8.2 presents descriptive statistics on the key variables considered.

128   *Public sector technology transfer*

Table 8.2   Descriptive statistics on key variables (n = 1,658)

Variable	Mean	Standard Deviation	Minimum	Maximum
USTechnologySales	0.104	0.305	0	1
Employment	30.744	59.352	1	460
Award	694 561	311,442	17,590	7,341,253
PrevPhII	0.903	2.138	0	28
PreviousPhII	0.396	0.489	0	1
PhaseIII	0.537	0.499	0	0
DOD	0.473	0.499	0	1
NIH	0.254	0.435	0	1
NASA	0.095	0.293	0	1
DOE	0.088	0.283	0	1
NSF	0.090	0.287	0	1

Note: DOD refers to the U.S. Department of Defense, NIH refers to the U.S. National Institutes of Health, NASA refers to the U.S. National Aeronautics and Space Administration, DOE refers to the U.S. Department of Energy, NSF refers to the U.S. National Science Foundation.

Held constant in the empirical analysis to describe across Phase II project differences in the sale of technology rights is the number of employees in the firm at the time of the Phase II proposal (a measure of human capital and firm size), the amount of the Phase II award in $2001 (a measure of technical capital), the number of previous Phase II awards to the firm for research on a technology related to the current Phase II project (also a measure of technical capital), and the presence of Phase III development funds. Funding agency effects are also considered.

The Probit results from this exploratory analysis of the likelihood of the firm engaging in technology transfer through the sale of technology rights to another U.S. firm or U.S. investor are in Table 8.3.

*Table 8.3   Probit regression results, dependent variable is
                USTechnologySales (n = 1,658) (p-values in parentheses,
                marginal effects in brackets)*

Variable	(1)	(2)
ln(Employment)	−0.081 [−0.014] (p = .009)	−0.08 [−0.014] (p = .009)
ln(Award)	0.029 [0.005] (p = .824)	−0.080 [0.005] (p = .831)
PrevPhII	0.029 [0.005] (p = .132)	–
PreviousPhII	–	0.252 [0.043] (p = .004)
PhaseIII	0.501 [0.082] (p < .0001)	0.478 [0.082] (p < .0001)
Agency effects	yes	yes
Wald χ^2	49.27 (p < .0001)	55.93 (p < .0001)

Note: From Table 8.2, the largest value of *Award* is $7,341,253. That value is an outlier, but if deleted from the sampling population the marginal effect of *ln(Award)* remains insignificant. The correlation coefficient between *Employment* and *Award* is also insignificant with or without the outlier.

Because of the exploratory nature of this analysis, only directional relationships are discussed. Four findings are perhaps worth noting.

First, smaller-sized firms are more engaged in the sale of technology rights than larger-sized firms. Perhaps smaller-sized firms lack the internal expertise to bring a new technology to market even with Phase III funding.

Second, the amount of the Phase II award is not related to the likelihood that a firm will sell its technology rights. Although the variables *Employment* and *Award* are not significantly correlated (rho = 0.006, p = .809), the apparent lack of internal expertise is the key explanatory resource.

Third, previous research experience related to the technology being sold is a positive covariate with *USTechnologySales*. Perhaps such experience conveys to other U.S. firms or U.S. investors a dimension of quality about the technology being sold. However, the number of previous awards (*PrevPhII*) is not a significant covariate, but the simple fact that the firm had received previous awards (*PreviousPhII*) is the key criterion.

Finally, those firms that received Phase III development funding are more likely to engage in the sale of their Phase II funded technology. Again, perhaps the presence of Phase III funding is also an indication of the quality of the Phase II technology.[2]

Not shown in Table 8.3 are the Probit results from alternative models, specifically models that included a binary variable measuring whether the project was commercialized. In no instance was a commercialization variable even marginally significant.

SUMMARY

In this chapter a new metric to quantify technology transfer from SBIR and STTR Phase II projects was considered, namely, the U.S. sale of the rights to Phase II project technology. Such a sale is indeed a technology transfer. Controlling for aspects of human capital and technical capital, a covariate with such sales is the presence of Phase III funding. Unfortunately, data are not available to suggest a counterfactual scenario, namely, how the firm would have transferred its technology in the absence of Phase III funding.

The following chapter builds on Chapter 7 by demonstrating empirically that SBIR (and STTR) *mills* do have a social benefit of transferring knowledge. Whether that activity is a net social benefit or not is, however, beyond the scope of the analysis in Chapter 9.

NOTES

1.   A few firms were at the time of the 2005 survey engaged in both finalized sales and ongoing negotiations.
2.   Information is not available as to whether the U.S. firm/investor that purchased the Phase II technology rights was also the firm/investor that provided Phase III development funding.

9. Knowledge transfers from SBIR mills

INTRODUCTION

In Feldman's testimony before the House Committee on Research and Technology Subcommittee, Committee on Science, Space, and Technology on April 6, 2022, she stated that the term *SBIR mills* is:[1]

> ... a pejorative term that implies that a significant number of [SBIR] awards go to a small number of small businesses who are dependent on government funding for their entire lifespan and do not end up commercializing anything.

While there is not a formal definition of an *SBIR mill*, perceptions about them abound, and those perceptions vary based on the accuracy of one's information.[2]

The Small Business Innovation Research (SBIR) (and Small Business Technology Transfer (STTR)) program was reauthorized through the SBIR and STTR Extension Act of 2022 (Public Law 117–183), signed by President Joseph Biden on September 30, 2022. As a result of Congressional concerns, the Act explicitly addressed mills under the legislated charge for funding agencies to "establish a due diligence program." Specifically:

> Not later than 18 months after the date of enactment of this Act, the Comptroller General of the United States shall conduct a study and submit to the Committee on Small Business and Entrepreneurship of the Senate and the Committee on Small Business and the Committee on Science, Space, and Technology of the House of Representatives a report, which shall be made publicly available, on small business concerns that are awarded not less than 50 Phase II awards under the SBIR or STTR programs during the consecutive period of 10 fiscal years preceding the most recent 2 fiscal years ...

Systematic empirical evidence about SBIR mills was recently published by Feldman et al. (2022). Therein, the authors document for 10 firms that account for more than 6 percent of all SBIR awards technology-related outputs from their funded research. The outputs considered are patents, publications, commercialized products, and the formation of spinoff companies.

In this chapter, I focus on patenting information from the NRC's 2005 Database which contains information on a random sample of firms funded through the SBIR programs of Department of Defense (DOD), National Institutes of Health (NIH), National Aeronautics and Space Administration (NASA), Department of Energy (DOE), and National Science Foundation (NSF) over the fiscal years 1992 thought 2001 (see Chapter 6).

DATABASE OF FUNDED FIRMS

The NRC's 2005 Database also includes a random sample of firms associated with the Phase II projects. Table 9.1 shows the number of responding firms in total and by funding agency.

Table 9.1   *Firms in the NRC 2005 Database*

	Number of Firms
All agencies	1,800
DOD	879
NIH	442
NASA	176
DOE	150
NSF	153

Note: DOD refers to the U.S. Department of Defense, NIH refers to the U.S. National Institutes of Health, NASA refers to the U.S. National Aeronautics and Space Administration, DOE refers to the U.S. Department of Energy, NSF refers to the U.S. National Science Foundation.
Source: NRC 2005 Database.

Among the survey questions asked was: *How many patents have resulted, at least in part, from your company's SBIR and/or STTR awards?* Table 9.2 shows the firms' response to this question in total and by agency. The research question asked is: *How do the number of patents differ between firms that are mills and those firms that are not?*

Table 9.2   *Patents received by firms in the NRC 2005 Database*

	Number of Patents Received
All agencies	12,756
DOD	6,877
NIH	1,343
NASA	2,155
DOE	1,204
NSF	1,177

Note: See Table 9.1 for agency abbreviations.
Source: NRC 2005 Database.

As stated above, there is no formal definition of a mill, be it a mill from SBIR awards or from STTR awards. For illustrative purposes, firms that are mills are defined here to be those in the right-hand side of the distribution of Phase I plus Phase II SBIR and STTR awards received.[3] Those firms that are in the top 10 percent of firms are defined herein as mills. Table 9.3 shows the number of so-defined firms.

Table 9.3   Firms in the NRC 2005 Database defined to be mills

	Number of Firms
All agencies	189
DOD	89
NIH	48
NASA	20
DOE	16
NSF	16

Note: See Table 9.1 for agency abbreviations.
Source: NRC 2005 Database.

EMPIRICAL ANALYSIS

To test for differences between firms defined to be mills and the other firms, I estimated a model with the number of patents (*NumberPatents*) as the dependent variable. The independent variables are the age of the firm at the time of the 2005 survey defined as (2005–*YearFounded*)—the range of values for the variable *YearFounded* is 1900 to 2001—if the firm is a mill or not (*Mill*); and binary agency controls. Table 9.4 shows the least-squares results from this model and the negative binominal results.

Table 9.4   *Regression results explaining across-firm differences in the number of patents received (p-values in parentheses) (n = 1,800)*

Variable	Least-Squares Coefficients	Negative Binominal Coefficients
YearFounded	−0.267 (p < .0001)	−0.014 (p = .002)
Mill	29.897 (p < .0001)	2.029 (p < .0001)
DOD	−0.161 (p = .894)	−0.392 (p = .002)
NIH	−4.500 (p = .0005)	−0.915 (p < .0001)
NASA	3.469 (p = .023)	0.001 (p =.994)
DOE	−0.324 (p = .838)	−0.112 (p = .505)
Intercept	534.94 (p < .0001)	29.042 (p = .001)
R²	0.379	–
Log Likelihood	–	26 508.12
Dispersion	–	1.955 (p < .0001)

Note: See Table 9.1 for agency abbreviations.

Based on either specification of the model, firms defined to be mills are associated with more patents, holding constant the age of the firm, than the other firms.

CONCLUSIONS

A recent commentary from the Niskanen Center stated:[4]

As we noted over the summer, SBIR mills capture a disturbingly high share of total awards, undermining the program's role as a springboard for genuine startups. In our piece, we argued that the simplest and more direct way to curb SBIR mills was to impose a lifetime cap on the number of awards a single business could win. It is not uncommon for an SBIR awardee to be engaged in multistage research that requires multiple awards and many years of work to achieve a viable product. There is no sound justification, however, for allowing a single firm to receive dozens or even hundreds of Phase I awards over the span of decades.

Perhaps the descriptive information in that chapter, which applied to both Phase I and Phase II awards, will expand thinking about the economic costs and benefits of mills. In their defense, mills are a source of knowledge as well as technology transfer.

NOTES

1. See https:// www .nationalacademies .org/ ocga/ testimony -before -congress/ sbir -turns-40-evaluating-support-for-small-business-innovation, accessed March 20, 2023.
2. The common term of use is *SBIR mills*, but some might claim that there are also STTR mills. The patent data considered in this chapter relate to both SBIR and STTR mills, but the title of the chapter conforms to the more commonly used term.
3. I have borrowed the distributional term from Feldman et al. (2022).
4. See https://www.niskanencenter.org/federal-aid-for-small-business-rd-is-getting -smarter-but-remains-too-easy-to-game/, accessed March 21, 2023.

10. Concluding statement

The purpose of this book is to provide analytical information (i.e., descriptive trends and statistical relationships) to characterize U.S. public sector technology transfer activities—activities that are publicly funded and publicly performed as well as those that are publicly funded and privately performed.

As a prelude to the descriptive analysis, a distinction between knowledge transfers and technology transfers was offered, as was some historical context about the concept of technology transfer. Critical to an appreciation of technology transfer trends in the United States is an understanding of the Nation's infrastructure that champions technology transfer from public sector agencies and laboratories. An historical overview of the Federal Laboratory Consortium (FLC) is, I believe, a hallmark chapter in this book.

From a pedagogical perspective, I divided the discussion between publicly funded publicly developed knowledge and technology transfers from publicly funded privately performed knowledge and technology transfers. To the best of my knowledge, the latter grouping of transfer has not previously been discussed under the umbrella of technology transfers as recently emphasized by both the Obama Administration and the Trump Administration.

With few exceptions, there are not generalizable conclusions to be made about the economic and social impact of the Great Recession on either knowledge transfers or technology transfers. Perhaps the story will have a different ending when future research is done on the economic and social impact of Covid-19 on knowledge and technology transfers.

I hope that the discussion in the previous chapters will stimulate additional research on knowledge and technology transfers in a direction that traces economic and social consequences. In other words, little is known about the impact on firms or organizations that use publicly developed knowledge and technology transfers. Case studies are certainly a starting point for understanding how firms or organizations benefit from licensed technologies from federal laboratories or from Cooperative Research and Development Agreement (CRADA) arrangement with federal laboratories. Equally important would be case studies of the consequences of firms or organizations utilizing technical knowledge absorbed through transfers from Small Business Innovation Research (SBIR) and Small Business Technology Transfer (STTR) Phase II projects.[1]

NOTE

1. One exemplary start in this direction is Feldman et al. (2022).

References

American Academy of Arts & Sciences (2020). *The Perils of Complacency: America at a Tipping Point in Science & Engineering*, Cambridge, MA: American Academy of Arts & Sciences.

Amoroso, Sara and Albert N. Link (2021). "Intellectual Property Protection Mechanisms and the Characteristics of Founding Teams," *Scientometrics*, 126: 7329–50.

Archibugi, Daniele, Andrea Filippetti, and Marion Frenz (2013). "The Impact of the Economic Crisis on Innovation: Evidence from Europe," *Technological Forecasting and Social Change*, 80: 1247–60.

Arrow, Kenneth J. (1962). "Economic Welfare and the Allocation of Resources for Invention," in *The Rate and Direction of Inventive Activity: Economic and Social Factors* (pp. 609–25), Princeton, NJ: Princeton University Press.

Audi, Robert (2002). "The Sources of Knowledge," in P.K. Moser (eds), *The Oxford Handbook of Epistemology* (pp. 71–94), New York: Oxford University Press.

Audretsch, David B. and Albert N. Link (2019). *Sources of Knowledge and Entrepreneurial Behavior*, Toronto: University of Toronto Press.

Bar-Zakay, Samuel N. (1971). "Policymaking Transfer: The Need for National Thinking Laboratories," *Policy Sciences*, 2: 213–27.

Bator, Francis M. (1958). "The Anatomy of Market Failure," *The Quarterly Journal of Economics*, 72: 351–79.

Bozeman, Barry and Albert N. Link (1983). *Investments in Technology: Corporate Strategies and Public Policy Alternatives*, New York: Praeger.

Bozeman, Barry and Albert N. Link (2014). "Toward an Assessment of Impacts from US Technology and Innovation Policies," *Science and Public Policy*, 43: 369–76.

Bozeman, Barry and Larry Wilson (2004). "Market-Based Management of Government Laboratories: The Evolution of the U.S. National Laboratories' Government-Owned, Contractor-Operated Management System," *Public Performance & Management Review*, 28: 167–85.

Brooks, Harvey (1996). "The Evolution of U.S. Science Policy," in B.L.R. Smith and C.E. Barfield (eds), *Technology, R&D, and the Economy* (pp. 15–48), Washington, DC: The Brookings Institution and American Enterprise Institute.

Bush, Vannevar (1945). *Science—the Endless Frontier: Report to the President*, Washington, DC: U.S. Government Printing Office. See also: https://slac.uconn.edu/wp-content/uploads/sites/2215/2019/10/Science-the-Endless-Frontier.pdf, accessed November 11, 2022.

Bush, Vannevar (1949). *Modern Arms and Free Men: A Discussion of the Role of Science in Preserving Democracy*, New York: Simon & Schuster.

Bush, Vannevar (1967). *Science Is Not Enough*, New York: William Morrow & Company.

Carnegie Mellon University (2017). *FFRDCs: A Primer*, Pittsburgh, PA: Carnegie Mellon University.

Carrillo, Francisco Javier (2022). *Knowledge: From Knowledge Economies to Knowledge in the Anthropocene*, Cheltenham, U.K and Northampton, MA, USA: Edward Elgar.

Cochrane, Rexmond C. (1966). *Measures for Progress: A History of the National Bureau of Standards*, Washington, DC: National Bureau of Standards.

Committee on Science and Technology (1979). *The Role of Federal Laboratories in Transferring Technology to State and Local Governments*, Washington, DC: Committee on Science and Technology.

Comptroller General of the United States (1979). "Interagency Laboratory Use: Current Practices and Recurring Problems," Washington, DC: General Accounting Office.

Comstock, Douglas A. and Daniel Lockney (2007). "NASA's Legacy of Technology Transfer and Prospects for Future Benefits," paper presented at the American Institute of Aeronautics and Astronautics SPACE 2007 Conference & Exposition, https://www.nasa.gov/pdf/330841main_aiaa_2007_6283_31.pdf, accessed November 30, 2022.

Congressional Research Service (CRS) (2021). "Science and Technology Issues in the 117th Congress," Washington, DC: Congressional Research Service.

Congressional Research Service (CRS) (2022). "Small Business Research Programs: SBIR and STTR," Washington, DC: Congressional Research Service.

Council of State Governments (1973). *Intergovernmental Uses of Federal R&D Centers and Laboratories*, Lexington, KY: Council of State Governments.

Czarnitzki, Dirk, Kornelius Kraft, and Susanne Thorwarth (2009). "The Knowledge Production of 'R' and 'D'," *Economics Letters*, 105: 141–3.

Dale, Bruce C. and Timothy D. Moy (2000). "The Rise of Federally Funded Research and Development Centers," Albuquerque, NM: Sandia National Laboratories.

Dalley, Stephanie (2008). *Myths from Mesopotamia: Creation, the Flood, Gilgamesh, and Others*, New York: Oxford University Press.

Doctors, Samuel I. (1969). *The Role of Federal Agencies in Technology Transfer*, Cambridge, MA: MIT Press.

Donald, Betsy, Meric S. Gertler, and Peter Tyler (2013). "Creatives after the Crash," *Cambridge Journal of Regions, Economy and Society*, 6: 3–21.

Eisenberg, Rebecca S. (1996). "Public Research and Private Development: Patents and Technology Transfer in Government-Sponsored Research," *Virginia Law Review*, 82: 1663–727.

Eisenstein, Elizabeth L. (1980). *The Printing Press as an Agent of Change: Communications and Cultural Transformations in Early Modern Europe* (2 Vols), New York: Cambridge University Press.

European Commission, Joint Research Centre (2020). *Knowledge Transfer Metrics: Towards a European-Wide Set of Harmonised Indicators*, Brussels: Luxembourg Publications Office of the European Union.

Federal Coordinating Council for Science, Engineering, and Technology (1977). *Directory of Federal Technology Transfer*, Washington, DC: U.S. Government Printing Office.

Federal Council for Science and Technology (1974). *Intergovernmental Use of Federal R&D Laboratories*, Washington, DC: U.S. Government Printing Office.

Federal Laboratory Consortium for Technology Transfer (FLC) (2018). *Federal Technology Transfer Legislation and Policy: The Green Book*, Washington, DC: Federal Laboratory Consortium.

Federal Laboratory Consortium for Technology Transfer (FLC) (2020). *Executive Board Guidebook*, Washington, DC: Federal Laboratory Consortium.

Feldman, Maryann, Evan E. Johnson, Remi Bellefleur, Savannah Dowden, and Eshika Talukder (2022). "Evaluating the Tail of the Distribution: The Economic Contributions of Frequently Awarded Government R&D Recipients," *Research Policy*, 51: 104539.

Gilmore, John S. and Charlton R. Price (1969). *The Environment and the Action in Technology Transfer 1970–1980*. Denver, CO: Denver Research Institute, University of Denver.

Government Accountability Office (GAO) (2014). "TECHNOLOGY TRANSFER: Federal Laboratory Consortium Should Increase Communication with Potential Customers to Improve Initiatives," Washington, DC: United States Government Accountability Office.

Government Accountability Office (GAO) (2018). "FEDERAL RESEARCH: Additional Actions Needed to Improve Licensing of Patented Laboratory Inventions," Report to the Chairman, Committee on the Judiciary, House of Representatives, Washington, DC: Government Accountability Office.

Hall, Bronwyn H. and Rosemarie Ham Ziedonis (2001). "The Patent Paradox Revisited: An Empirical Study of Patenting in the U.S. Semiconductor Industry, 1979–1995," *RAND Journal of Economics*, 32: 101–28.

Hall, Michael J., Albert N. Link, and Matthew Schaffer (2022). "An Economic Analysis of Standard Reference Materials," *Journal of Technology Transfer*: 47: 1847–60.

Harris, J.R. (1992). *Essays in Industry and Technology in the Eighteenth Century: England and France*. Brookfield, VT: Ashgate.

Hart, David M. (2014). "An Agent, Not a Mole: Assessing the White House Office of Science and Technology Policy," *Science and Public Policy*, 41: 411–18.

Hayter, Christopher S. and Albert N. Link (2022). "From Discovery to Commercialization: Accretive Intellectual Property Strategies among Small, Knowledge-Based Firms," *Small Business Economics*, 58: 1367–77.

Hayter, Christopher S., Albert N. Link, and Matthew Schaffer (2023). "Identifying the Emergence of Academic Entrepreneurship with the Technology Transfer Literature," *Journal of Technology Transfer*, 48: 1800–1812.

Hayter, Christopher S., Albert N. Link, and John T. Scott (2018). "Public-Sector Entrepreneurship," *Oxford Review of Economic Policy*, 34: 676–94.

Hébert, Robert F. and Albert N. Link (2009). *A History of Entrepreneurship*, New York: Routledge.

Hyman, Malcolm D. and Jürgen Renn (2012). "From Technology Transfer to the Origins of Science," in J. Renn (ed.), *The Globalization of Knowledge in History* (pp. 75–104), Berlin: Neopubli GmbH.

Inkster, Ian (2007). "Technology in World History: Cultures of Constraint and Innovation, Emulation, and Technology Transfers," *Comparative Technology Transfer and Society*, 5: 108–27.

Interagency Workgroup on Technology Transfer (IAWGTT) (2012). "Revised Technology Transfer Metrics in Response to the October 28, 2011 Presidential Memorandum: Accelerating Technology Transfer and Commercialization of Federal Research in Support of High-Growth Businesses," https://www.nist.gov/document/metricspaper-final-1–29–13pdf, accessed March 2, 2023.

Jolly, James A. and J.W. Creighton (1977). "The Technology Transfer Process: Concepts, Framework and Methodology," *Journal of Technology Transfer*, 1: 77–91.

Kevles, Daniel J. (1977). "The National Science Foundation and the Debate over Postwar Research Policy," *Isis*, 68(241): 5–26.

Latker, Norman J. (2000). "Brief History of Federal Technology Transfer," Testimony before Advisory Committee of the National Institute for General Medical Sciences, https://ipmall.law.unh.edu/sites/default/files/BAYHDOLE/latkinPDF/Brief_History_of_Federal_Technology_Transfer_by_Norman_J._Latker,_9–24–2000.pdf, accessed November 30, 2022.

Leyden, Dennis Patrick and Albert N. Link (2015). *Public Sector Entrepreneurship: U.S. Technology and Innovation Policy*, New York: Oxford University Press.

Lindsell, Harold (1971). *The Holy Bible*. Revised Standard Version, Grand Rapids, MI: Zondervan Publishing House.

Link, Albert N. (2006). *Public/Private Partnerships: Innovation Strategies and Policy Alternatives*, New York: Springer.

Link, Albert N. (2021). "Knowledge Transfers from Federally Funded Research and Development Centers," *Science and Public Policy*, 48: 576–81.

Link, Albert N. (2022a). *The Economics and Science of Measurement: A Study of Metrology*, London: Routledge.

Link, Albert N. (2022b). "Vannevar Bush: A Public Sector Entrepreneur," *Foundations and Trends in Entrepreneurship*, 18: 1–74.

Link, Albert N. (2023a). "The Economics of Metrology: An Exploratory Study of the Impact of Measurement Science on U.S. Productivity," *Economics of Innovation and New Technology*, 32: 213–22.

Link, Albert N. (2023b). "The U.S. Small Business Technology Transfer (STTR) Program: An Assessment and an Evaluation of the Program," *Annals of Science and Technology Policy*, 7: 81–151.

Link, Albert N. and James Cunningham (2021). *Advanced Introduction to Technology Policy*, Cheltenham, U.K. and Northampton, MA, USA: Edward Elgar.

Link, Albert N. and Zachary T. Oliver (2020). *Technology Transfer and US Public Sector Innovation*, Cheltenham, U.K. and Northampton, MA, USA: Edward Elgar.

Link, Albert N. and John T. Scott (2011). *Public Goods, Public Gains: Calculating the Social Benefits of Public R&D*, New York: Oxford University Press.

Link, Albert N. and John T. Scott (2012). *Employment Growth from Public Support of Innovation in Small Firms*, Kalamazoo, MI: W.E. Upjohn Institute for Employment Research.

Link, Albert N. and Martijn van Hasselt (2019). "On the Transfer of Technology from Universities: The Impact of the Bayh-Dole Act of 1980 on the Institutionalization of University Research," *European Economic Review*, 119: 472–81.

Link, Albert N. and Martijn van Hasselt (2020). "Exploring the Impact of R&D on Patenting Activity in Small Women-Owned and Minority-Owned Entrepreneurial Firms," *Small Business Economics*, 54: 1061–6.

Link, Albert N. and Martijn van Hasselt (2022). "The Use of Intellectual Property Protection Mechanisms by Publicly Supported Firms," *Economics of Innovation and New Technology*, 31: 111–21.

Link, Albert N. and Martijn van Hasselt (2023). *Small Firms and U.S. Technology Policy: Social Benefits of the U.S. Small Business Innovation Research Program*, Cheltenham, U.K. and Northampton, MA, USA: Edward Elgar.

Link, Albert N. and Caroline S. Wagner (2021). "The Publicness of Publicly Funded Research," *Science and Public Policy*, 48: 757–62.

Link, Albert N., Cody A. Morris, and Martijn van Hasselt (2019). "The Impact of Public R&D Investments on Patenting Activity: Technology Transfer at the U.S. Environmental Protection Agency," *Economics of Innovation and New Technology*, 28: 536–46.

Link, Albert N., Christopher A. Swann, and Martijn van Hasselt (2022). "An Assessment of the U.S. Small Business Innovation Research (SBIR) Program: A Study of Project Failure," *Science and Public Policy*, 49: 972–8.

Linsteadt, George F. (1976). "Department of Defense Technology Transfer Consortium: An Overview," *Journal of Technology Transfer*, 1: 107–17.

Linsteadt, George F. (1978). "Federal Laboratory Consortium for Technology Transfer: A National Resource," *The Space Congress® Proceedings*, pp. 21–8.

Locke, John (1996). *An Essay Concerning Human Understanding* (edited by K.P. Winkler), Cambridge, MA: Hackett Publishing Company.

Martin, Benton C. (2009). "The American Models of Technology Transfer: Contextualized Emulation by Developing Countries?" *Buffalo Intellectual Property Law Journal*, 6: 101–29.

McDougall, Walter A. (1985). *The Heavens and the Earth: A Political History of the Space Age*, Baltimore, MD: Johns Hopkins University Press.

Medema, Steven G. (2007). "The Hesitant Hand: Mill, Sidgwick, and the Evolution of the Theory of Market Failure," *History of Political Economy*, 39: 331–58.

Metcalf, Harold (1994). "Lessons from History: Origins of the Federal Laboratory Consortium for Technology Transfer," *Journal of Technology Transfer*, 19: 13–17.

Miller, Gerald E. (1979). "Testimony for the House Subcommittee on Science, Research, and Technology," in Committee on Science and Technology, *The Role of Federal Laboratories in Transferring Technology to State and Local Governments* (pp. 44–5), Washington, DC: Committee on Science and Technology.

National Academies of Sciences, Engineering, and Medicine (2016). *STTR: An Assessment of the Small Business Technology Transfer Program*, Washington, DC: The National Academies Press.

National Academies of Science, Engineering, and Medicine (2022). *Ontologies in the Behavioral Sciences: Accelerating Research and the Spread of Knowledge*, Washington, DC: The National Academies Press.

National Academy of Engineering (1974). *Technology Transfer and Utilization: Recommendations for Redirecting the Emphasis and Correcting the Imbalance*, Washington, DC: U.S. Government Printing Office.

National Institute of Standards and Technology (NIST) (2019). "Return on Investment Initiative for Unleashing American Innovation," *NIST Special Publication 1234*, Gaithersburg, MD: U.S. National Institute of Standards and Technology.

National Institute of Standards and Technology (NIST) (2022). "Federal Laboratory Technology Transfer: Fiscal Year 2020," Gaithersburg, MD: National Institute of Standards and Technology.

National Research Council (2008). *An Assessment of the SBIR Program*, Washington, DC: The National Academies Press.

National Research Council (2011). *Measuring the Impacts of Federal Investments in Research*, Washington, DC: The National Academies Press.

National Science and Technology Council (2021). *National Strategic Overview for Research and Development Infrastructure*, Washington, DC: Executive Office of the President of the United States.

Noh, Heeyong and Sungjoo Lee (2019). "Where Technology Transfer Research Originated and Where It Is Going: A Quantitative Analysis of Literature Published between 1980 and 2015," *Journal of Technology Transfer*, 44: 700–40.

Office of Technology Assessment (OTA, 1995). *A History of the Department of Defense Federally Funded Research and Development Centers, OTA-BP-ISS-157*. Washington, DC: U.S. Government Printing Office.

Potts, Daniel T. (2012). "Technological Transfer and Innovation in Ancient Eurasia," in J. Renn (ed.), *The Globalization of Knowledge in History* (pp. 105–23), Berlin: Neopubli GmbH.

President's Management Agenda (undated). https://www.performance.gov/PMA/PMA .html, accessed November 26, 2022.

Rasberry, Stanley D. (2003). *Standard Reference Materials—the First Century*, NIST Report 260–150, Gaithersburg, MD: National Institute of Standards and Technology.

Roland, Alex (1992). "Secrecy, Technology, and War: Greek Fire and the Defense of Byzantium, 678–1204," *Technology and Culture*, 33: 655–79.

Rosenberg, Nathan (1970). "Economic Development and the Transfer of Technology: Some Historical Perspectives," *Technology and Culture*, 11: 550–75.

Rudolph, Lawrence (1994). "Overview of Federal Technology Transfer," *Risk*, 5: 133–41.

Samuelson, Paul A. (1954). "The Pure Theory of Public Expenditure," *The Review of Economics and Statistics*, 36: 387–9.

Schooley, James F. (2000). *Responding to National Needs: The National Bureau of Standards Becomes the National Institute of Standards and Technology, 1969—1993*, Gaithersburg, MD: National Institute of Standards and Technology.

Schultz, Theodore W. (1975). "The Value of the Ability to Deal with Disequilibria," *Journal of Economic Literature*, 13, 827–846.

Seely, Bruce Edsall (2003). "Historical Patterns in the Scholarship of Technology Transfer," *Comparative Technology Transfer and Society*, 1: 7–48.

Seely, Bruce Edsall (2008). "NASA and Technology Transfer in Historical Perspective," *Comparative Technology Transfer and Society*, 6: 1–16.

Shackle, G.L.S. (1966). *The Nature of Economic Thought*, Cambridge: Cambridge University Press.

Sivertsen, Gunnar, Ronald Rousseau, and Lin Zhang (2019). "Measuring Scientific Contributions with Modified Fractional Counting," *Journal of Informetrics*, 13: 679–94.

Snyder, Belinda and Jeffrey W. Thomas (undated). "GOGOs, GOCOs, and FFRDCs … Oh My!?" https://www.federallabs.org/download/file/fid/23628, accessed October 14, 2023.

Stewart, Robert K. (1993). "The Office of Technical Services: A New Deal Idea in the Cold War," *Knowledge*, 15: 44–77.

Swann, G.M. Peter (2009). "The Economics of Metrology and Measurement," Report for National Measurement Office, Department for Business, Innovation and Skills, London.

Task Force on Science Policy, Committee on Science and Technology, House of Representatives (1986). *A History of Science Policy in the United States, 1940–1985*, Washington, DC: U.S. Government Printing Office.

Teich, Albert H. (1979). "Statement of Dr. Albert H. Teich," in Committee on Science and Technology, *The Role of Federal Laboratories in Transferring Technology to State and Local Governments* (pp. 1–12), Washington, DC: Committee on Science and Technology.

The Economist (2002). "Innovation's Golden Goose," December 14, p. 3.

Tuma, Elias H. (1987). "Technology Transfer and Economic Development: Lessons of History," *The Journal of Developing Areas*, 21: 403–28.

United Nations Educational, Scientific and Cultural Organization (UNESCO) (1968). *National Science Policies of the U. S. A: Origins, Development and Present Status*, Paris: UNESCO.

U.S. Department of Commerce (USDOC) (2019). *Annual Report on Technology Transfer: Approach and Plans, Fiscal Year 2019 Activities and Achievements, U.S. Department of Commerce*, Gaithersburg, MD: National Institute of Standards and Technology.

U.S. Department of Commerce (USDOC) (2020). *Guidance for Preparing Annual Agency Technology Transfer Reports*, Gaithersburg, MD: National Institute of Standards and Technology.

Wiesner, J.B. (1979). "Vannevar Bush," in National Academy of Sciences (ed.), *Biographical Memoirs* (Vol. 50, pp. 89–117), Washington, DC: The National Academy Press.

Zachary, G. Pascal (1997). *Endless Frontier: Vannevar Bush, Engineer of the American Century*, New York: Free Press.

Index

Founding Fathers 2, 15
fractional counting 40
Franklin, Benjamin 44
free competition 98
funding agency effects 128

Gage, Lyman 39
GOCO model *see* government-owned,
  contractor-operated model
GOGO model *see* government-owned,
  government-operated model
government agencies, World War II 4
government-owned, contractor-operated
  (GOCO) model 58, 97
government-owned,
  government-operated (GOGO)
  model 58
government role, direct versus indirect
  2–4
Great Recession 9, 136
  calibration testing 22–4, 26
  creative responses 23, 92, 124
  defensive publishing 124
  SBIR/STTR awards 106
  SRM sales 28
  technology transfer mechanisms/
    metrics 79, 81, 83–6, 92, 96
The Green Book 4

Hall, Michael J. 28
Hatch Act 46–7
Hatch, William H. 60
Hayter, Christopher S. 47, 124
Hébert, Robert F. 18, 24, 96
human capital
  disequilibrium situations 24
  R&D projects 2, 14
  research outputs 19
  technology rights sales 128, 130
  university resources 123
human resources 89–90, 92, 94
Hyman, Malcolm D. 43

IAWGTT *see* Interagency Working
  Group on Technology Transfer
ideas, genesis of 17–19
indirect role, government 3–4
industrial organizations 97
information sharing behavior 2, 15

innovation
  descriptions of 115
  for economic growth 1, 9, 13
  knowledge transfer for 12–13
  small businesses 98–9, 104
intellectual property 34, 113
intellectual property protection
  mechanism (IPPM) 124
Interagency Working Group on
  Technology Transfer (IAWGTT)
  8–10, 71, 97
invention, definition 92
invention disclosures 92–6
invention licenses 72, 75, 77–9, 84–5, 90
IPPM *see* intellectual property protection
  mechanism

Jankowski, John 112
Jefferson, Thomas 3, 44–5
joint ventures 103
Journal of Technology Transfer (JTT)
  35–8, 41

keywords
  consolidation process 36
  use of term 36–7, 41
Kilgore, Harley 4, 53–4
knowledge
  definitions 15
  embodiment of 115
  inward/outward flows 50
  as public good 2–3
  sources of 17–19, 39
  systematic applications 99
knowledge capital 39
knowledge channels 20
knowledge development 34, 45
knowledge spillovers 21
knowledge transfer (KT) 5, 17–41,
  114–25
  characterization of 114
  early U.S. activity 44–7
  economic benefits 26, 114
  examples 20–38
  incentivizing 50
  for innovation 12–13
  invention disclosures 92–6
  metrics 12–13
  S&E article trends 30